JEFFREY SELLER   SANDER JACOBS   JILL FURMAN

AND

THE PUBLIC THEATER

PRESENT

H★MILTON

AN AMERICAN MUSICAL

BOOK, MUSIC AND LYRICS BY

LIN-MANUEL MIRANDA

INSPIRED BY THE BOOK *ALEXANDER HAMILTON* BY
RON CHERNOW

WITH

DAVEED DIGGS   RENÉE ELISE GOLDSBERRY   JONATHAN GROFF   CHRISTOPHER JACKSON
JASMINE CEPHAS JONES   LIN-MANUEL MIRANDA   JAVIER MUÑOZ   LESLIE ODOM, JR.
OKIERIETE ONAODOWAN   ANTHONY RAMOS   PHILLIPA SOO

AND

CARLEIGH BETTIOL   ANDREW CHAPPELLE   ARIANA DEBOSE   ALYSHA DESLORIEUX
SYDNEY JAMES HARCOURT   NEIL HASKELL   SASHA HUTCHINGS   THAYNE JASPERSON
STEPHANIE KLEMONS   MORGAN MARCELL   EMMY RAVER-LAMPMAN
JON RUA   AUSTIN SMITH   SETH STEWART   BETSY STRUXNESS
EPHRAIM SYKES   VOLTAIRE WADE-GREENE

SCENIC DESIGN	COSTUME DESIGN	LIGHTING DESIGN	SOUND DESIGN
DAVID KORINS	PAUL TAZEWELL	HOWELL BINKLEY	NEVIN STEINBERG

HAIR AND WIG DESIGN	MUSIC COORDINATOR	PRESS REPRESENTATIVE
CHARLES G. LAPOINTE	MICHAEL KELLER MICHAEL AARONS	SAM RUDY MEDIA RELATIONS

TECHNICAL SUPERVISION	PRODUCTION STAGE MANAGER	COMPANY MANAGER
HUDSON THEATRICAL ASSOCIATES	J. PHILIP BASSETT	BRIG BERNEY

CASTING	ARRANGEMENTS	GENERAL MANAGEMENT
TELSEY + COMPANY BETHANY KNOX, CSA	ALEX LACAMOIRE LIN-MANUEL MIRANDA	BASELINE THEATRICAL ANDY JONES

MUSIC DIRECTION AND ORCHESTRATIONS BY

ALEX LACAMOIRE

CHOREOGRAPHY BY

ANDY BLANKENBUEHLER

DIRECTED BY

THOMAS KAIL

THE WORLD PREMIERE OF HAMILTON WAS PRESENTED IN NEW YORK IN FEBRUARY 2015 BY THE PUBLIC THEATER.
OSKAR EUSTIS, ARTISTIC DIRECTOR   PATRICK WILLINGHAM, EXECUTIVE DIRECTOR

ISBN 978-1-4950-5754-0

EXCLUSIVELY DISTRIBUTED BY

7777 W. BLUEMOUND RD. P.O. BOX 13819 MILWAUKEE, WI 53213

Visit Hal Leonard Online at
www.halleonard.com

Lin-Manuel Miranda is an Emmy, Grammy, and Tony Award-winning composer, lyricist, and performer, and a 2015 MacArthur Foundation Award recipient. *Hamilton*, for which he wrote the book, music and lyrics in addition to originating the title role, opened on Broadway in 2015 following a sold-out run at New York's Public Theater. Its Original Broadway Cast Recording won the 2016 Grammy Award for Best Musical Theater Album. Off-Broadway, *Hamilton* received a record-breaking 10 Lortel Awards, 3 Outer Critic Circle Awards, 8 Drama Desk Awards, the New York Drama Critics Circle Award for Best New Musical, and an OBIE for Best New American Play. Material from the show was previewed at the White House during its first-ever Evening of Poetry & Spoken Word in 2009.

Miranda's first Broadway musical, *In the Heights*, received four 2008 Tony Awards (Best Score, Best Orchestrations, Best Choreography and Best Musical), as well as Miranda's nomination for Best Leading Actor in a Musical. The show won a 2009 Grammy for its Original Broadway Cast Album and was recognized as a Finalist for the 2009 Pulitzer Prize in Drama.

Miranda is the co-composer and co-lyricist of Broadway's *Bring It On: The Musical* (2013 Tony nomination for Best Musical; 2013 Drama Desk nomination for Best Lyrics in a Musical). He contributed new songs to the revival of Stephen Schwartz' *Working*, as well as Spanish translations for the 2009 Broadway Revival of *West Side Story*.

Miranda won an Emmy Award as the lyricist of the 2013 Tony Awards opening number, "Bigger." He is the co-founder of the hip-hop improv group Freestyle Love Supreme. Miranda is the recipient of the ASCAP Foundation's Richard Rodgers New Horizons Award and the National Arts Club Medal of Honor. A graduate of Wesleyan University, he lives in New York City with his wife, son, and dog.

Special thanks to:

Jonny Baird

Nolan Bonvouloir

Brian Barone

Kurt Crowley

Khiyon Hursey

Adam Michael Kaufman

Madeline Myers

Scott Wasserman

Ian Weinberger

Will Wells

Rachael Ziering

ALEXANDER HAMILTON

Words and Music by LIN-MANUEL MIRANDA
Arranged by Alex Lacamoire and Lin-Manuel Miranda

JEFFERSON:

lot smart-er, by be-ing a self-start-er, by four-teen, they placed him in charge of a trad-ing char-ter. And

ev-'ry day while slaves were be-ing slaugh-tered and cart-ed a-way____ a-cross the waves, he strug-gled and kept his guard up. In-

MADISON:

side, he was long-ing for some-thing to be a part of, the broth-er was read-y to beg, steal,__ bor-row or bar-ter. Then a

hur-ri-cane came, and dev-as-ta-tion reigned, our man____ saw his fu-ture drip, drip-ping down the drain, put a

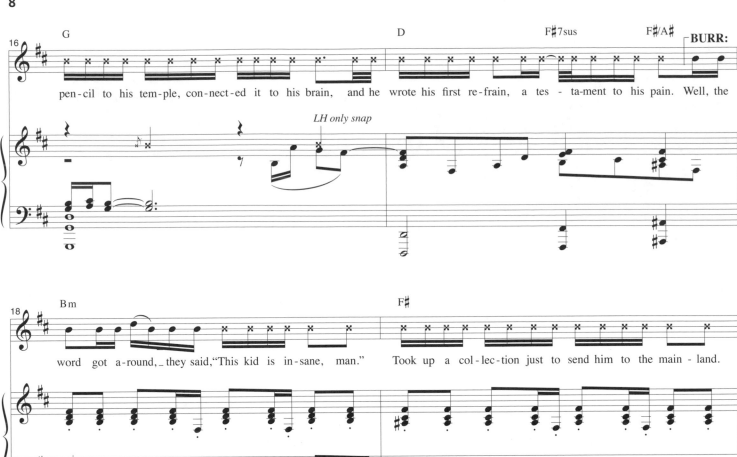

pen-cil to his tem-ple, con-nect-ed it to his brain, and he wrote his first re-frain, a tes - ta-ment to his pain. Well, the

word got a-round, _ they said, "This kid is in-sane, man." Took up a col-lec-tion just to send him to the main - land.

"Get your ed-u-ca-tion, don't for-get from whence you came, and the world is gon-na know your name. What's your name, man?"

HAMILTON:

Al - ex - an - der Ham - il - ton. My name is Al - ex - an - der Ham - il - ton. And there's a

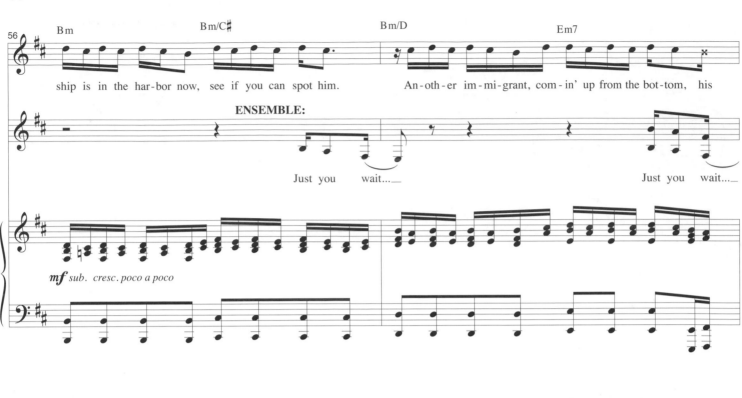

ship is in the har-bor now, see if you can spot him.

An-oth-er im-mi-grant, com-in' up from the bot-tom, his

ENSEMBLE:

Just you wait...

Just you wait...

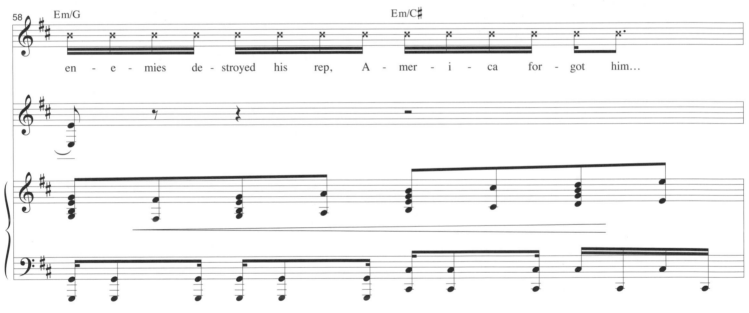

en - e - mies de - stroyed his rep, A - mer - i - ca for-got him...

MULLIGAN/MADISON/LAFAYETTE/JEFFERSON: LAURENS/PHILIP: WASHINGTON: ELIZA/ANGELICA/PEGGY/MARIAH: BURR:

We fought with him. Me? I died for him. Me? I trust - ed him. Me? I loved him. And me?

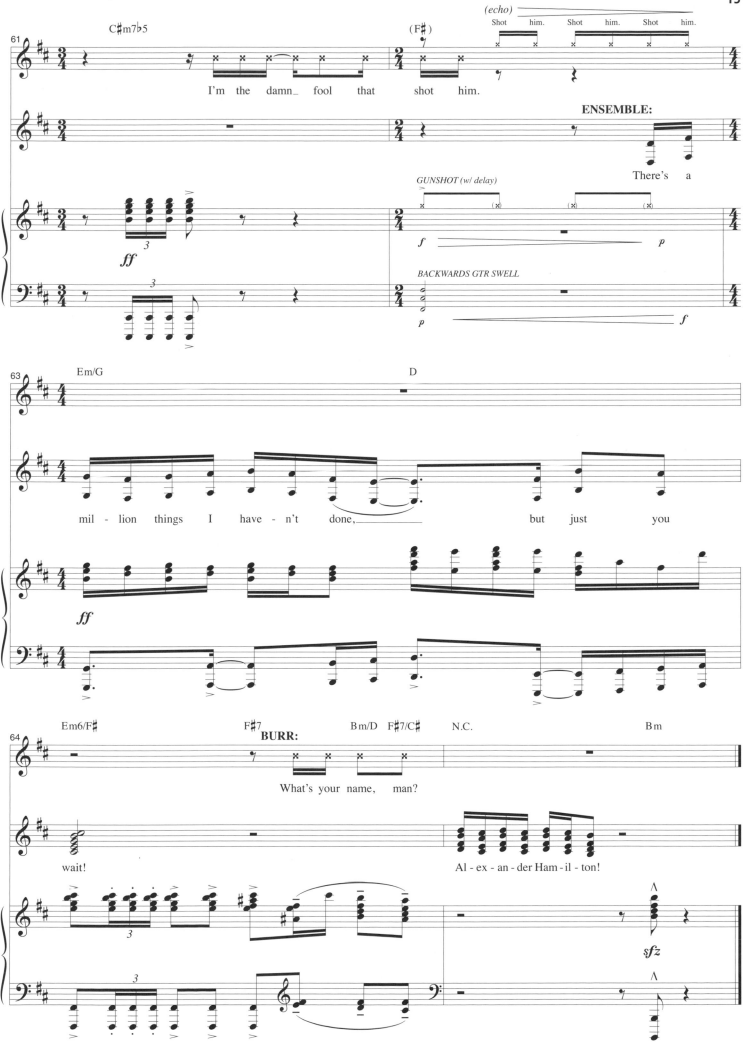

MY SHOT

Words and Music by LIN-MANUEL MIRANDA
with Albert Johnson, Kejuan Waliek Muchita,
Osten Harvey, Jr., Roger Troutman, Christopher Wallace
Arranged by Alex Lacamoire and Lin-Manuel Miranda

7 scholar-ship to King's Col-lege. I prob-'ly should-n't brag, but dag, I a-maze and a-ston-ish. The prob-lem is I got a

9 lot of brains but no pol-ish. I got-ta hol-ler just to be heard. With ev-er-y word, I drop knowl-edge! I'm

11 dia-mond in the rough, a shin-y piece of coal tryin' to reach my goal. My pow-er of speech: un-im-peach-a-ble.

13 On-ly nine-teen but my mind is old-er. These New York Cit-y streets get cold-er, I shoul-der ev-'ry

MULLIGAN: my shot! Yo, I'm a tail-or's ap-pren-tice, and I got y'all knu-ckle-heads *in lo-co par-en-tis.* I'm

HAMILTON/LAURENS/MULLIGAN: Shot!

joi-ning the re-bel-lion_ 'cause I know it's my chance_ to so-cial-ly ad-vance,_ in-stead of sew-in' some pants!_ I'm gon-na

LAURENS: take a shot! But we'll nev-er be tru-ly free un-til those in bon-dage have the same rights as you and me, you

HAMILTON/LAFAYETTE/LAURENS: Shot!

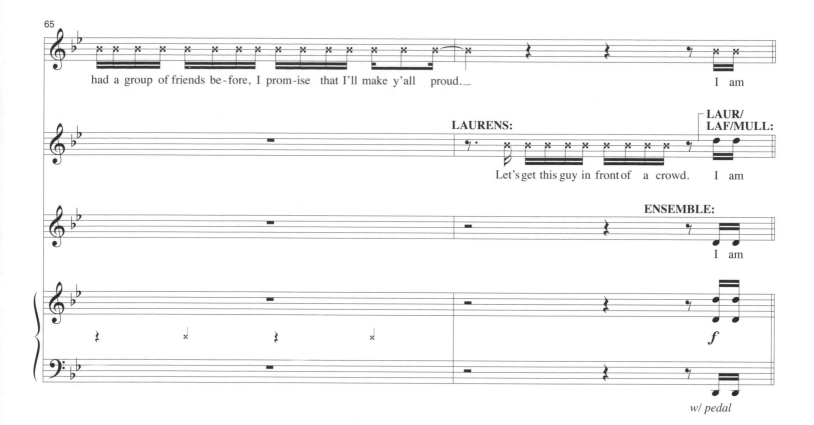

had a group of friends be-fore, I prom-ise that I'll make y'all proud.__ I am

LAURENS:
Let's get this guy in front of a crowd.

LAUR/ LAF/MULL:
I am

ENSEMBLE:
I am

f

w/ pedal

Gm   F/A   Bb   G7/B

not throw-ing a-way my shot. I am not throw-ing a-way my shot. Hey yo, I'm

not throw-ing a-way my shot. I am not throw-ing a-way my shot. Hey yo, I'm

not throw-ing a-way my shot. I am not throw-ing a-way my shot. Hey yo, I'm

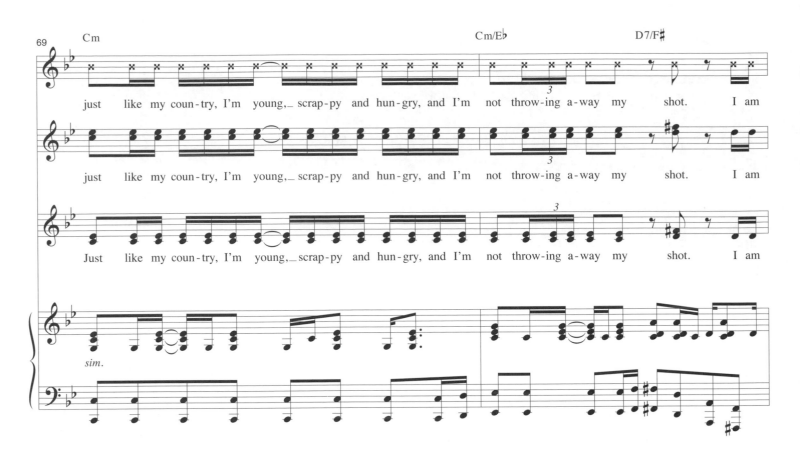

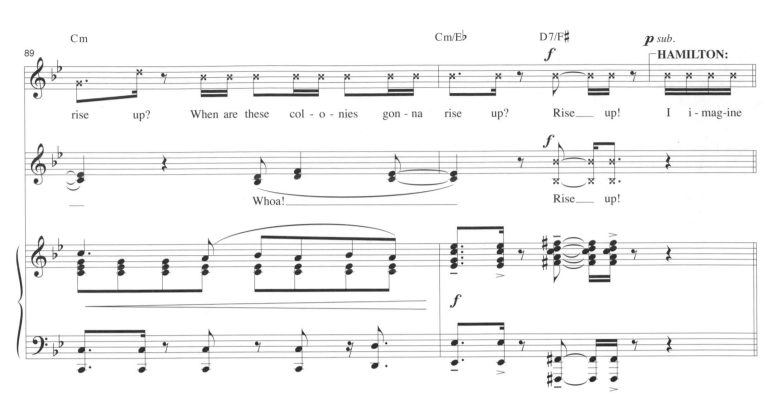

rise up? When are these col - o - nies gon - na rise up? Rise___ up! I i - mag-ine

Whoa!_____ Rise___ up!

HAMILTON:

Meno mosso

death so much it feels more like a mem - o - ry. When's it gon - na get me? In my sleep? Sev - en feet a - head of me?

"SCOTTISH SNARE" LOOP

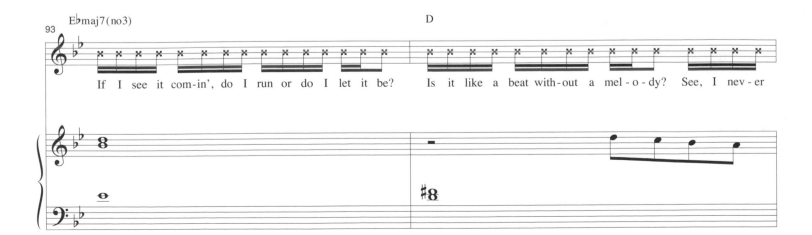

If I see it com - in', do I run or do I let it be? Is it like a beat with - out a mel - o - dy? See, I nev - er

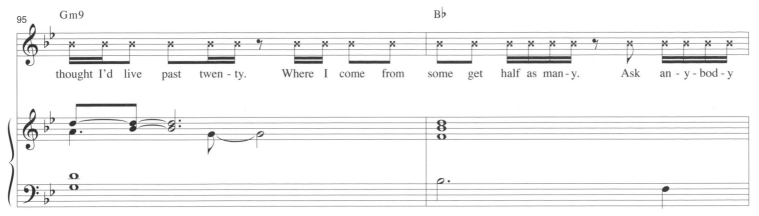

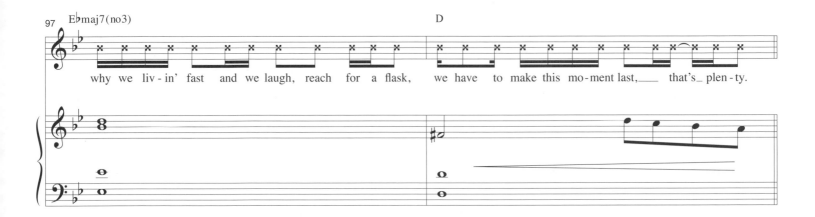

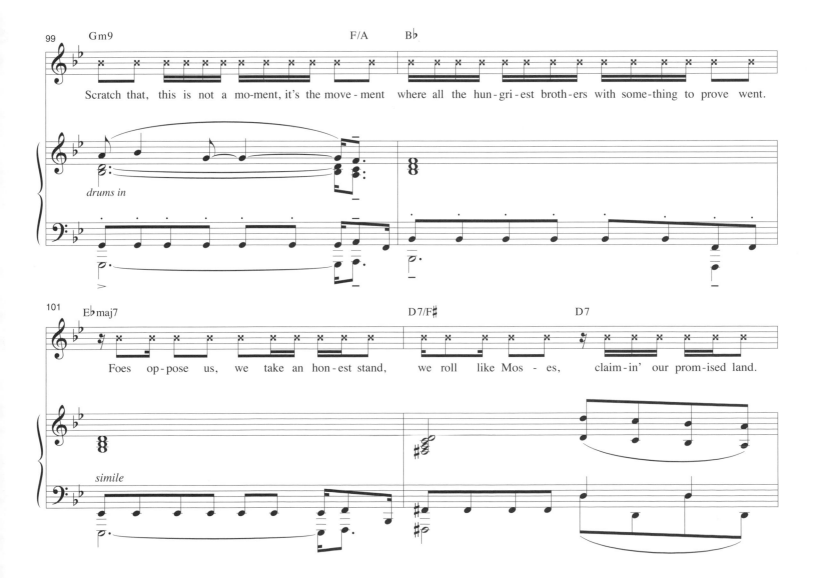

And? If we win our in-de-pen-dence? 'Zat a guar-an-tee of free-dom for our de-scen-dants?

Or will the blood we shed__ be-gin an end-less cy-cle of ven-geance and death__ with no de-fen-dants?

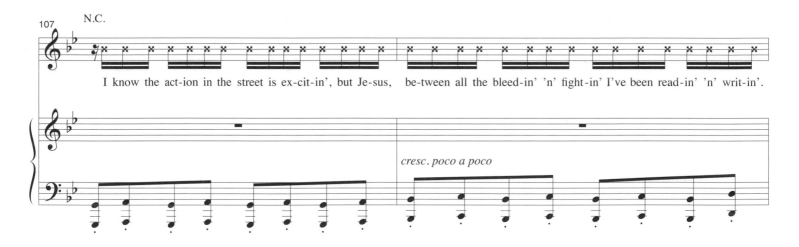

I know the act-ion in the street is ex-cit-in', but Je-sus, be-tween all the bleed-in' 'n' fight-in' I've been read-in' 'n' writ-in'.

cresc. poco a poco

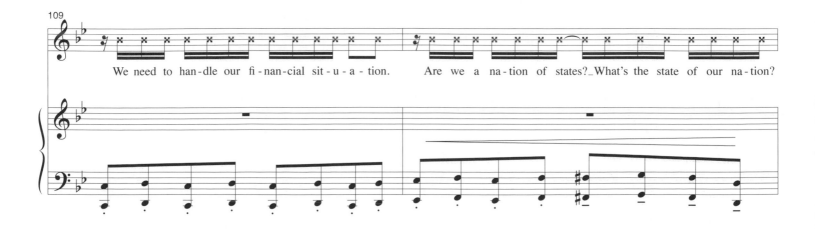

We need to han-dle our fi-nan-cial sit-u-a-tion. Are we a na-tion of states?__ What's the state of our na-tion?

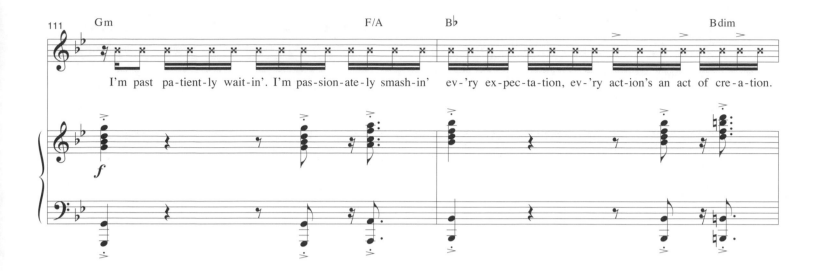

I'm past pa-tient-ly wait-in'. I'm pas-sion-ate-ly smash-in' ev-'ry ex-pec-ta-tion, ev-'ry act-ion's an act of cre-a-tion.

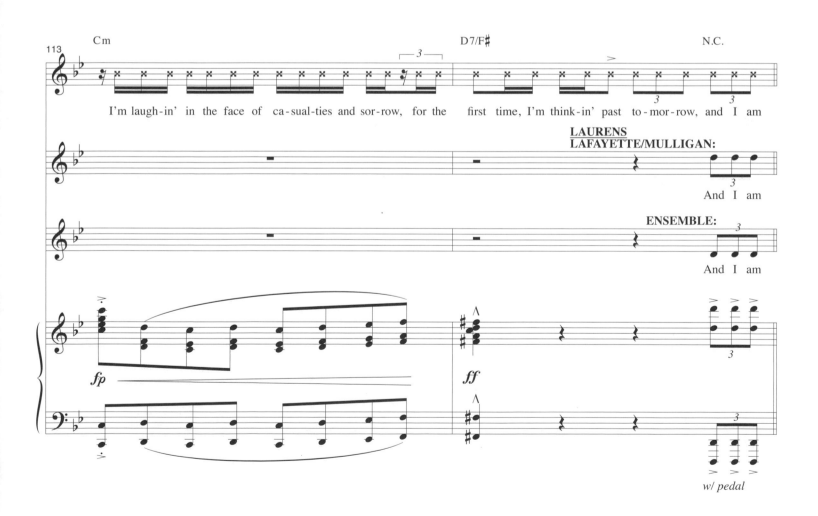

I'm laugh-in' in the face of ca-sual-ties and sor-row, for the first time, I'm think-in' past to-mor-row, and I am

LAURENS
LAFAYETTE/MULLIGAN:
And I am

ENSEMBLE:
And I am

w/ pedal

THE SCHUYLER SISTERS

Words and Music by LIN-MANUEL MIRANDA
Arranged by Alex Lacamoire and Lin-Manuel Miranda

Funky (♩ = 102)

OLD-SCHOOL VINYL HIT

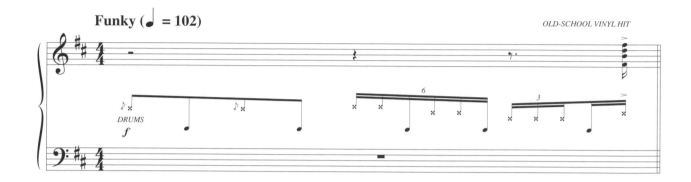

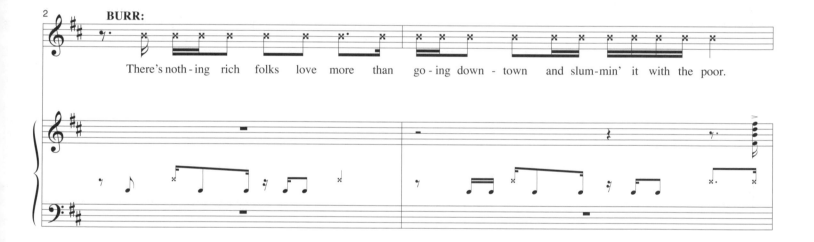

BURR: There's noth-ing rich folks love more than go-ing down-town and slum-min' it with the poor.

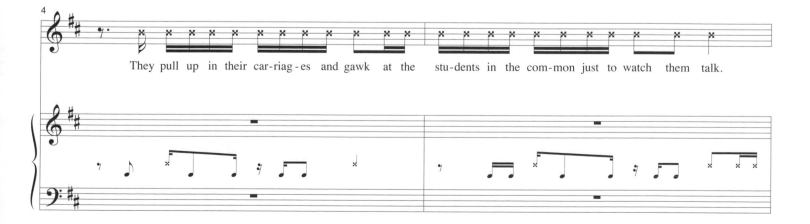

They pull up in their car-riag-es and gawk at the stu-dents in the com-mon just to watch them talk.

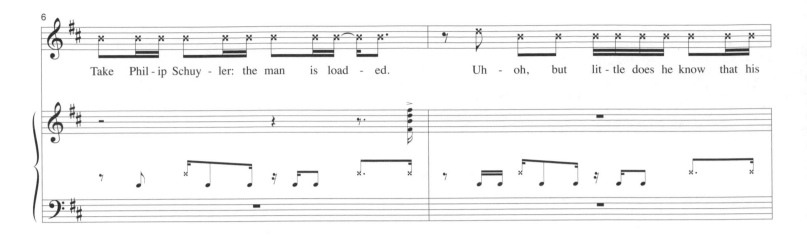

Take Phil-ip Schuy-ler: the man is load-ed. Uh-oh, but lit-tle does he know that his

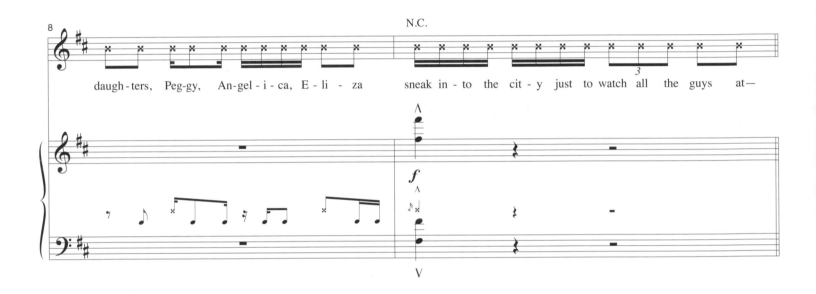

daugh-ters, Peg-gy, An-gel-i-ca, E-li-za sneak in-to the cit-y just to watch all the guys at—

ANGELICA: An-gel-i-ca!

PEGGY: And

ELIZA: E-li-za!

ENSEMBLE: Work, work! Work, work!

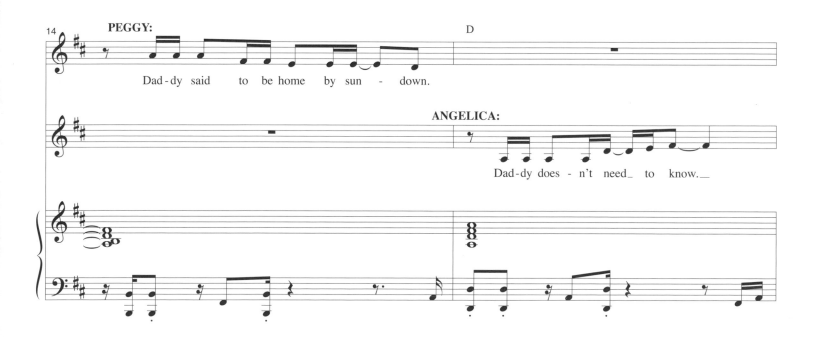

YOU'LL BE BACK

Words and Music by LIN-MANUEL MIRANDA
Arranged by Alex Lacamoire and Lin-Manuel Miranda

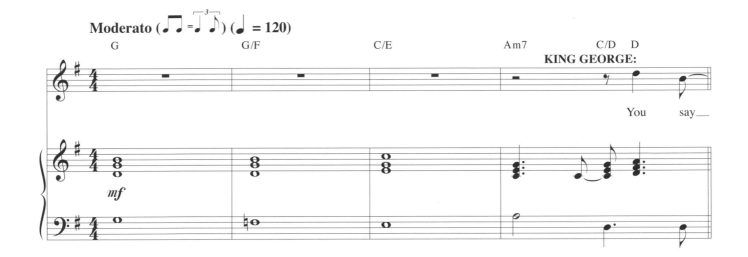

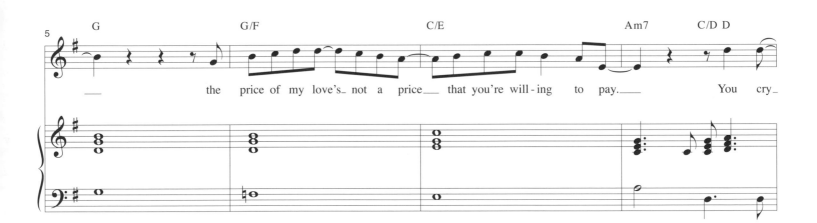

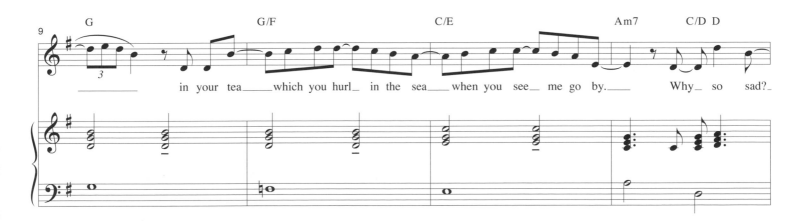

Re - mem-ber we made__ an ar-range - ment when you__ went a - way,__

__ now you're mak - ing me mad.__ Re - mem-ber, de - spite__ our es - trange -

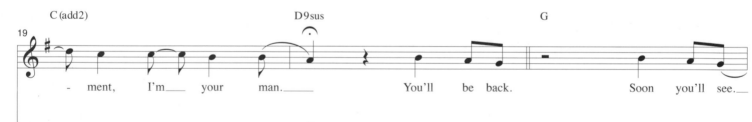

- ment, I'm__ your man.__ You'll be back. Soon you'll see.__

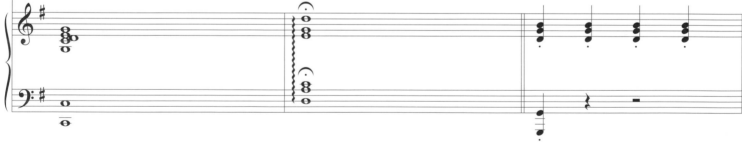

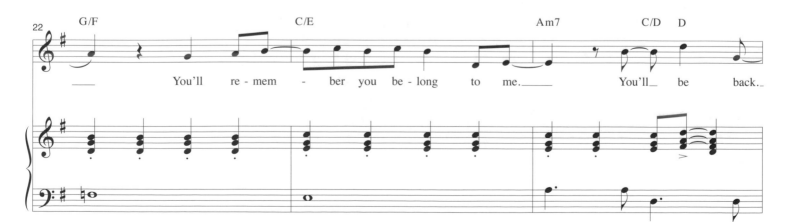

__ You'll re - mem - ber you be - long to me.__ You'll__ be back.__

Time_ will tell.___ You'll re-mem - ber that I served you well.___ O - ceans rise,_

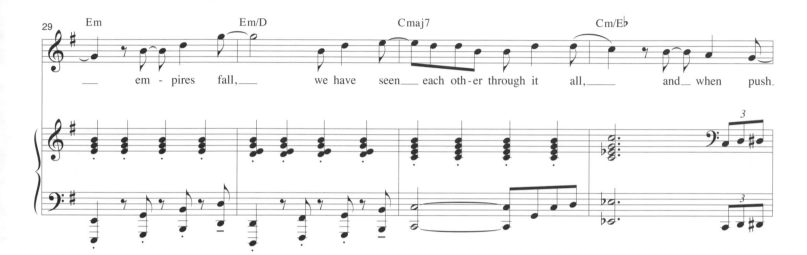

_ em - pires fall,___ we have seen___ each oth-er through it all,___ and_ when push_

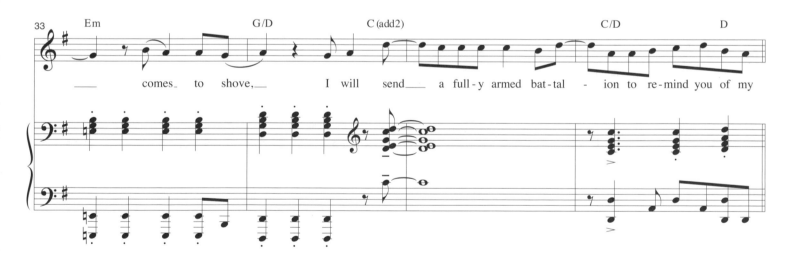

_ comes_ to shove,___ I will send___ a full-y armed bat-tal - ion to re-mind you of my

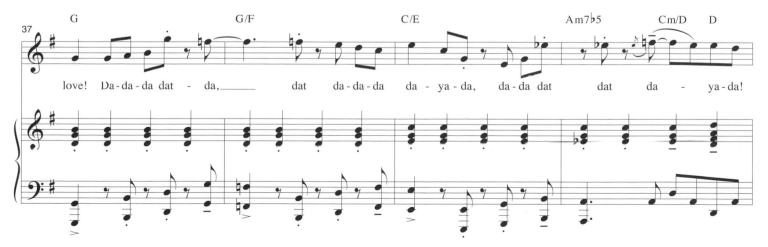

love! Da-da-da dat - da,___ dat da-da-da da-ya-da, da-da dat dat da - ya-da!

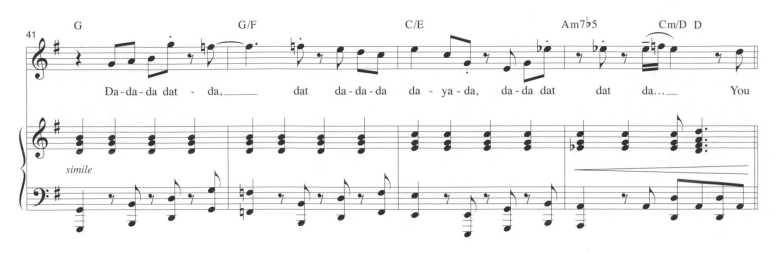

Da-da-da dat - da,_____ dat da-da-da da-ya-da, da-da dat dat da...____ You

say__ our love__ is drain-ing and you can't go on._____ You'll

be__ the one__ com - plain-ing when__ I am gone..._____ And

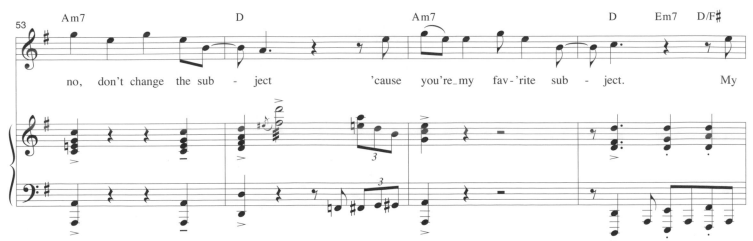

no, don't change the sub - ject 'cause you're__ my fav-'rite sub - ject. My

sweet, sub-mis-sive sub - ject, my loy-al, roy - al sub - ject, for-ev - er and ev - er and ev - er and ev - er and ev - er... You'll be back, like be - fore.___ I will fight___ the fight and win the war___ for___ your love,___ for___ your praise,___ and I'll love___ you till my dy - ing days.___ When___ you're gone___

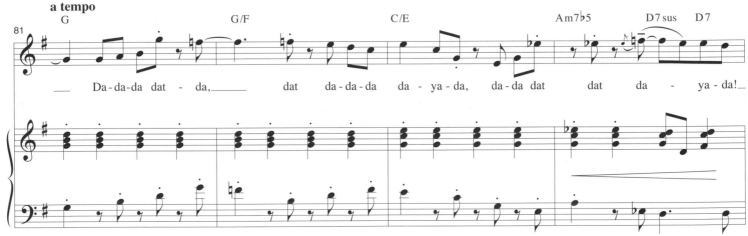

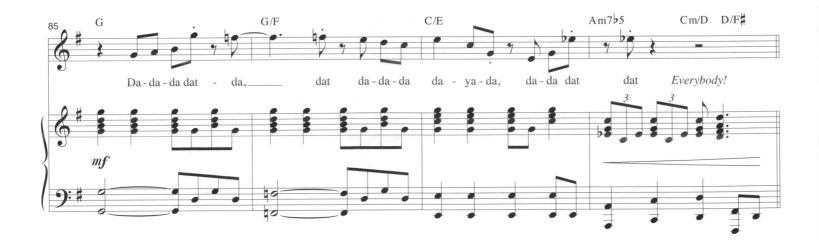

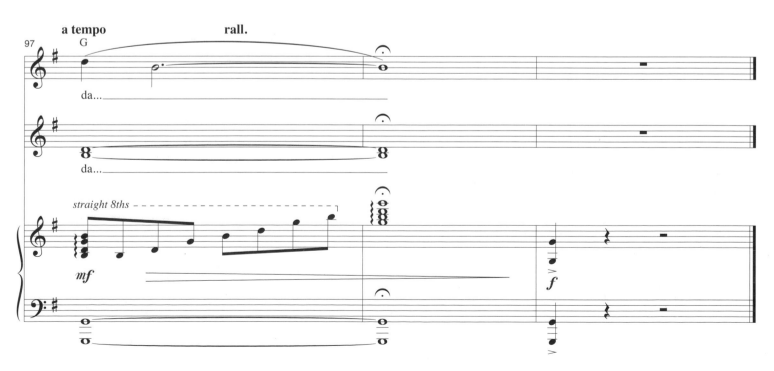

HELPLESS

Words and Music by LIN-MANUEL MIRANDA
Arranged by Alex Lacamoire and Lin-Manuel Miranda

Light, with a bounce; Swing 16ths (♩ = 79)

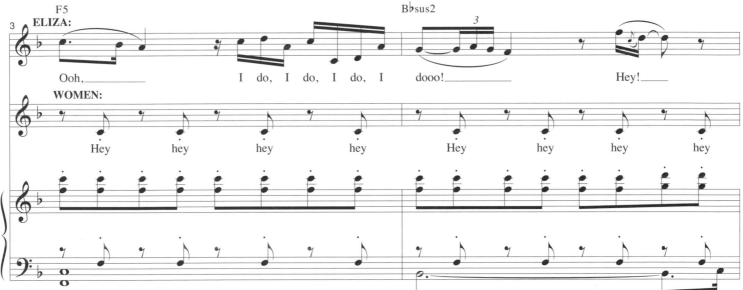

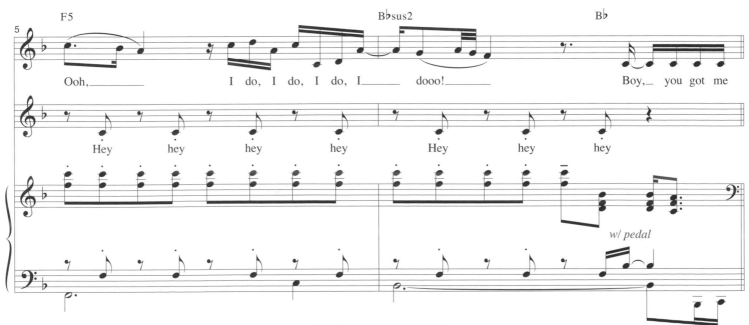

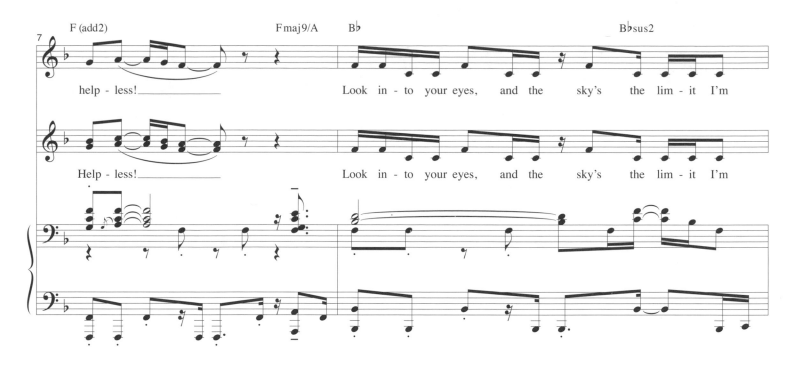

help - less!_____ Look in - to your eyes, and the sky's the lim - it I'm

Help less!_____ Look in - to your eyes, and the sky's the lim - it I'm

help - less!_____ Down for the count, and I'm drown - in' in 'em.

help - less!_____ Down for the count, and I'm drown - in' in 'em.

ELIZA:

I have nev - er been the type to try and grab the spot - light. We were at a rev - el with some reb - els on a hot night,

no pedal

laugh-in' at my sis-ter as she's daz-zl-ing the room, then you walked in and my heart went "boom"!

Tryin' to catch your eye from the side of the ball-room, ev-'ry-bod-y's danc-in' and the band's top vol-ume,

Grind to the rhy-thm as we wine and dine.__ Grab my sis-ter, and whis-per, "Yo, this one's mine."

ENS. WOMEN:

Grind to the rhy-thm as we wine and dine.__

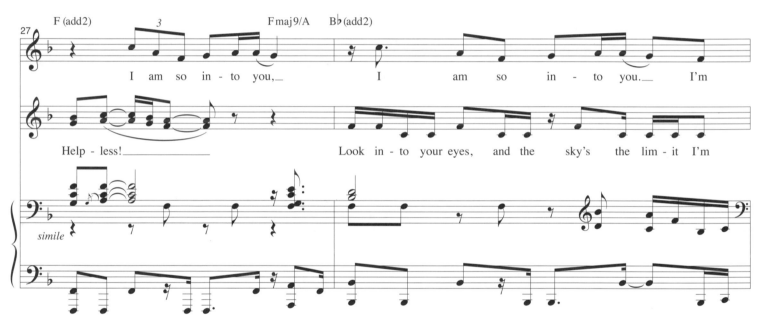

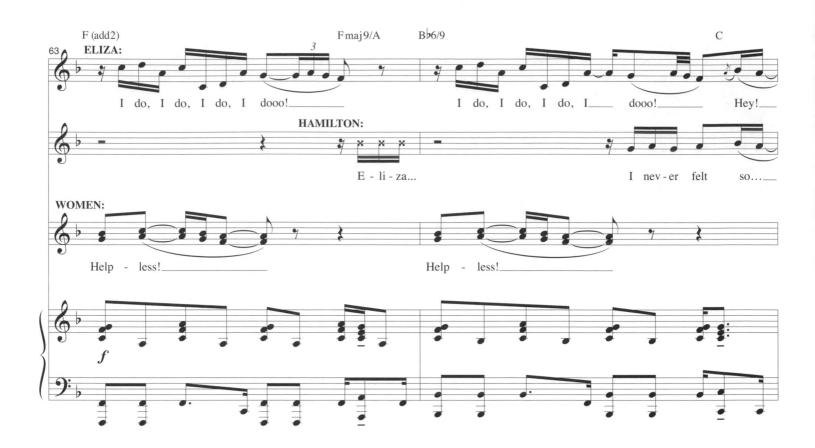

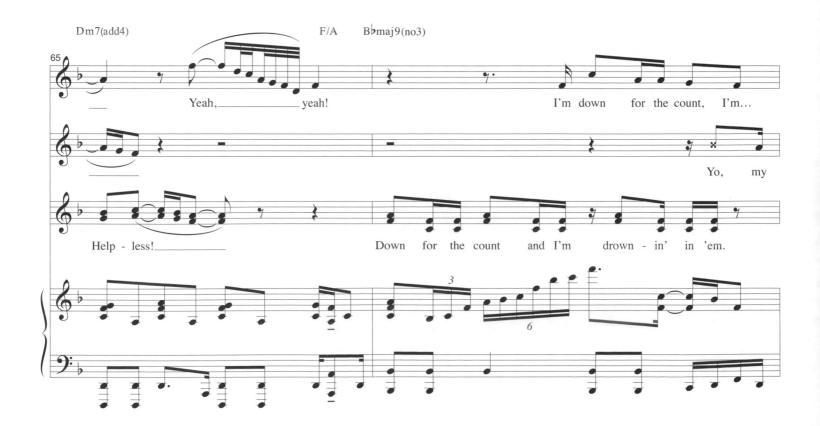

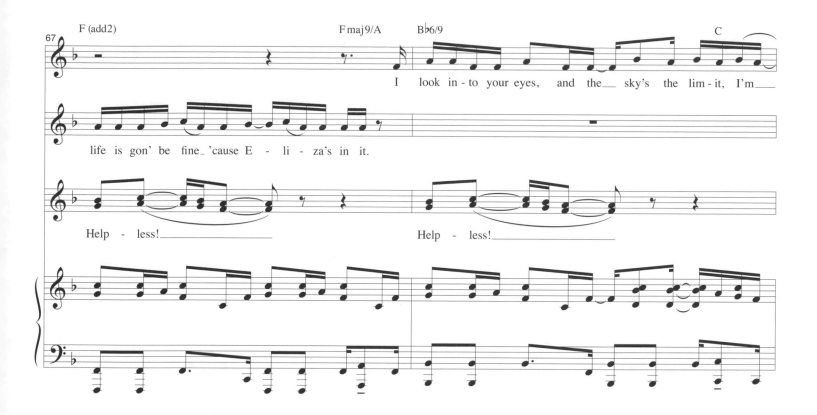

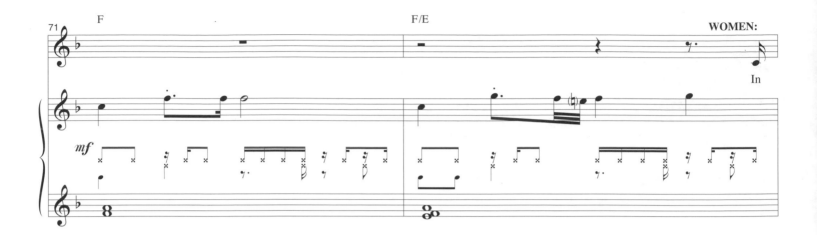

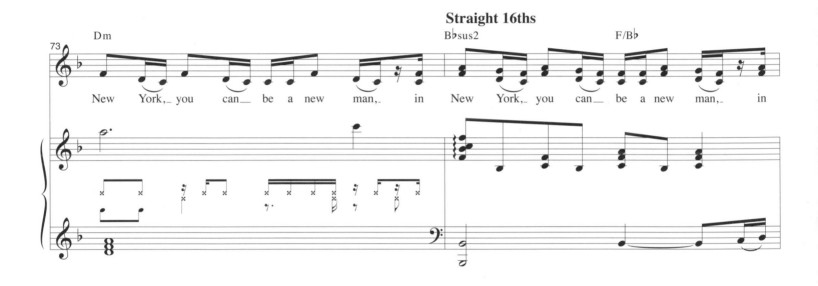

SATISFIED

Words and Music by LIN-MANUEL MIRANDA
Arranged by Alex Lacamoire and Lin-Manuel Miranda

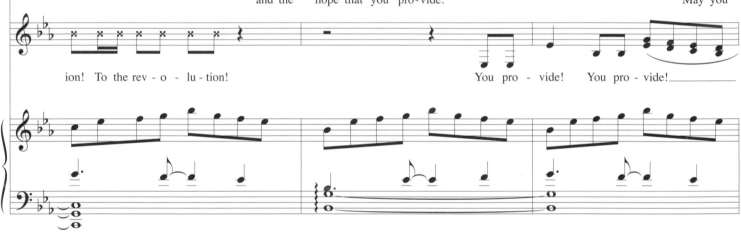

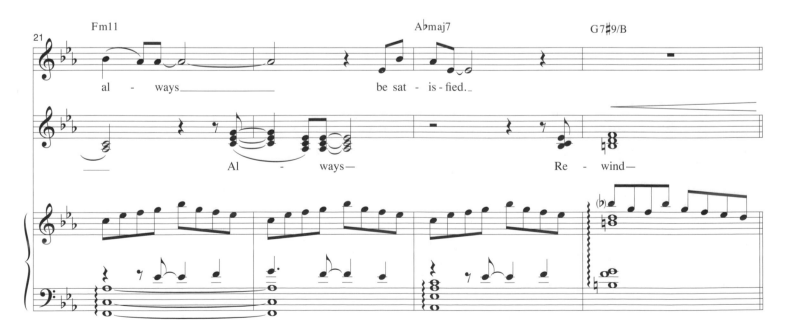

face.___ I have nev-er been the same. In - tel - li - gent eyes___ in a

hun - ger-pang frame,___ and when you said "Hi,"___ I for - got my dang name,___ set my

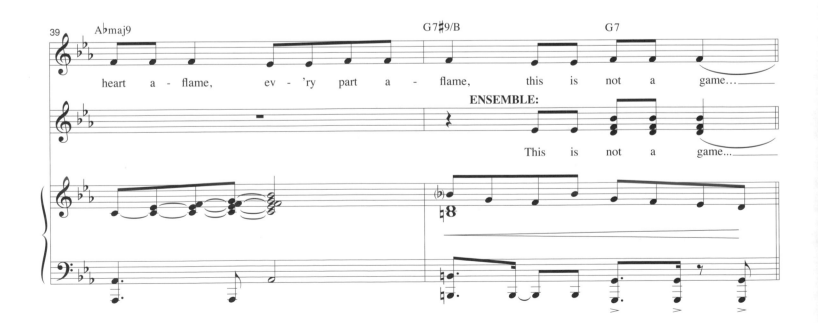

heart a - flame, ev - 'ry part a - flame, this is not a game...___

ENSEMBLE:

This is not a game...___

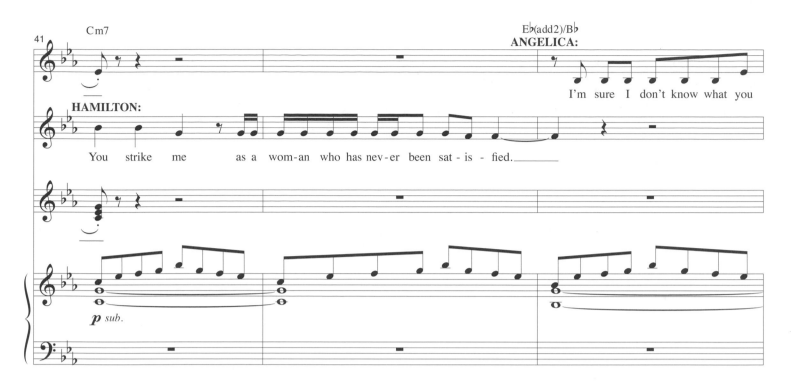

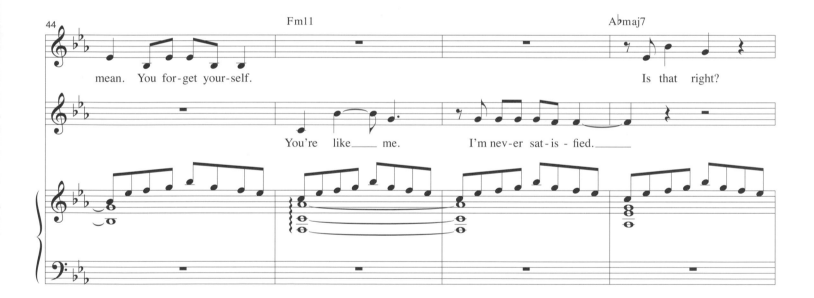

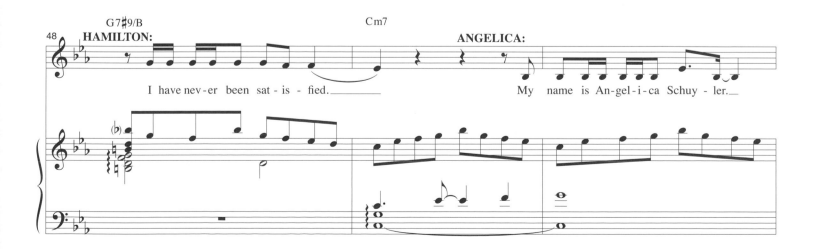

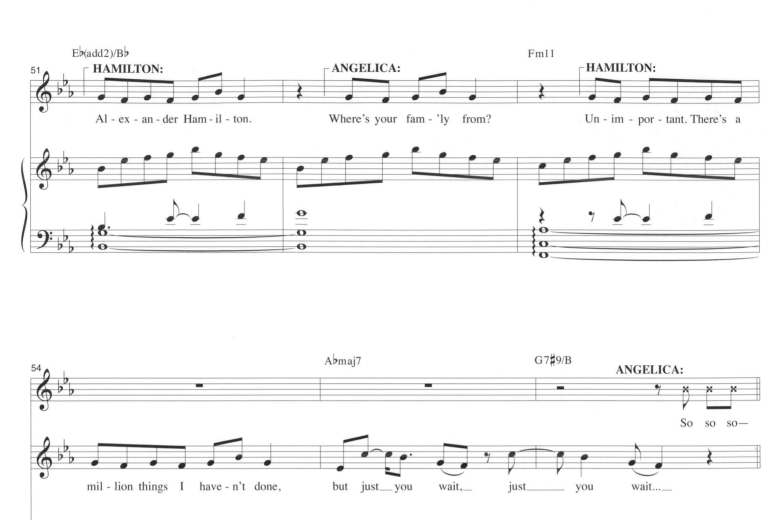

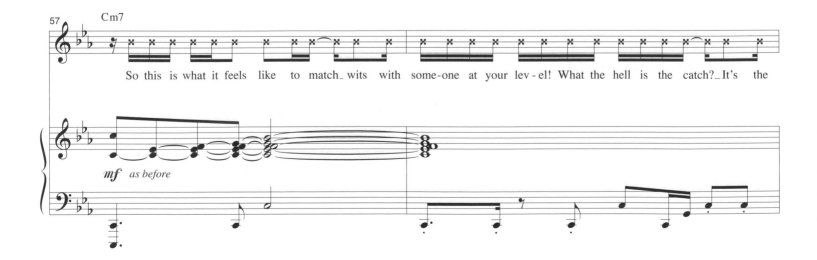

old - est and the wit - ti - est and the gos - sip in New York Cit - y is in - sid - i - ous.

Al - ex - an - der is pen - ni - less. Ha! That does - n't mean I want him an - y less. **ENSEMBLE:** Num - ber

ANGELICA: two! He's af - ter me __ 'cause I'm a Schuy - ler sis - ter. That el - e - vates his stat - us, I'd have to be na - ïve to set that

a - side, may - be that is why I in - tro - duce him to E - li - za, now that's his bride.

Nice go-ing, An-gel-i-ca, he was right,___ you will nev-er be sat-is-fied.

ENSEMBLE:

Num - ber

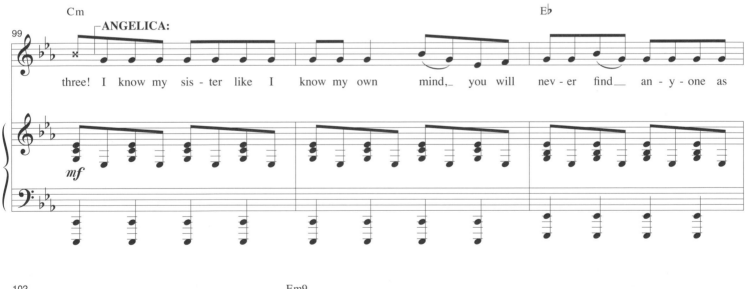

ANGELICA:

three! I know my sis-ter like I know my own mind,_ you will nev-er find__ an-y-one as

trust-ing or as kind._ If I tell her that I love him she'd be si-lent-ly re-signed,_ he'd be__

WAIT FOR IT

Words and Music by LIN-MANUEL MIRANDA
Arranged by Alex Lacamoire and Lin-Manuel Miranda

Allegro; with restrained intensity (♩ = 188)

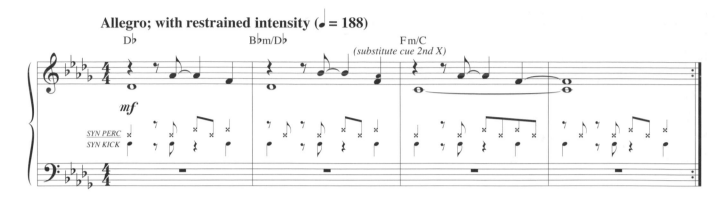

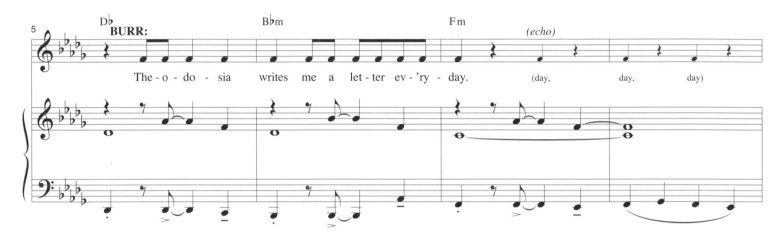

The-o-do-sia writes me a let-ter ev-'ry day. (day, day, day)

I'm keep-ing her bed warm while her hus-band is a-way. (way, way, way)

He's on the Brit-ish side in Geor-gia. He's tryin' to keep the col-o-nies in line.

He can keep_ all of Geor-gia. The-o-do - sia, she's_ mine. Love_

_ does-n't dis-crim-i-nate be-tween the sin-ners and the saints, it takes and it takes and it takes and we_

_ keep lov-ing an-y-way. We laugh and we cry and we break and we make our mis-takes. And if_

_ there's a rea-son I'm_ by her side when so_ man-y have tried then I'm_ will-ing to

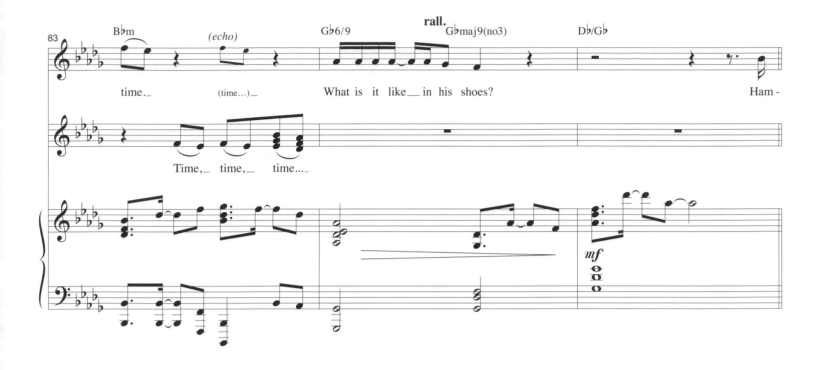

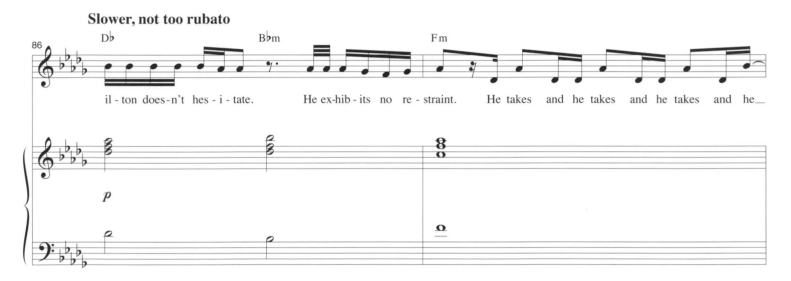

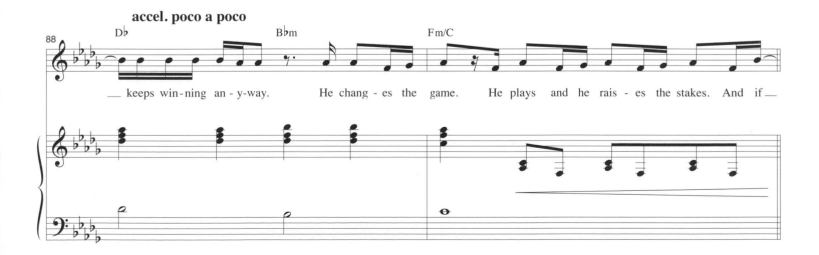

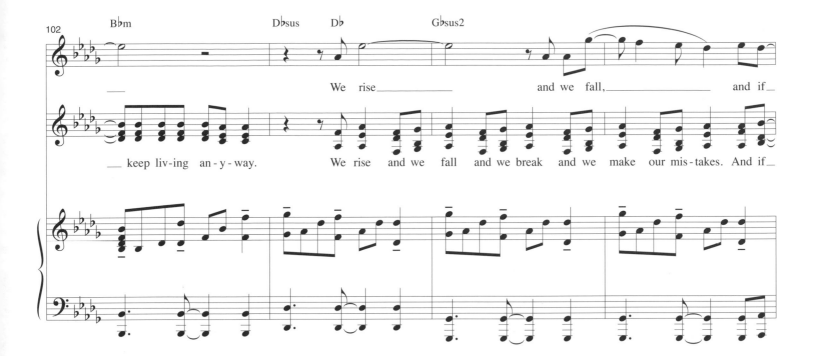

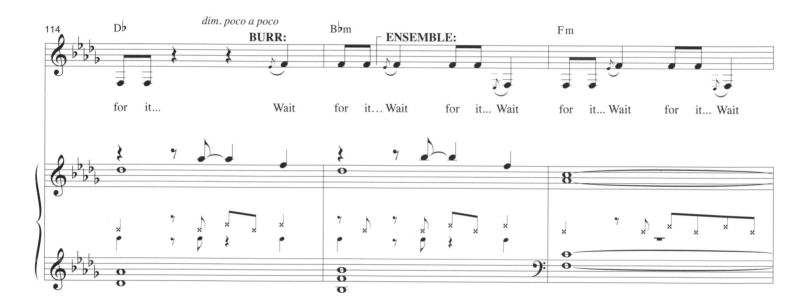

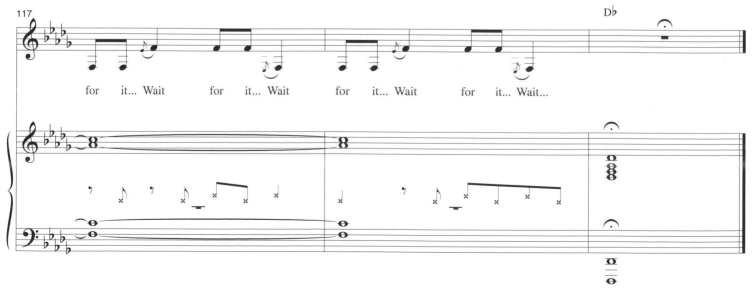

THAT WOULD BE ENOUGH

Words and Music by LIN-MANUEL MIRANDA
Arranged by Alex Lacamoire and Lin-Manuel Miranda

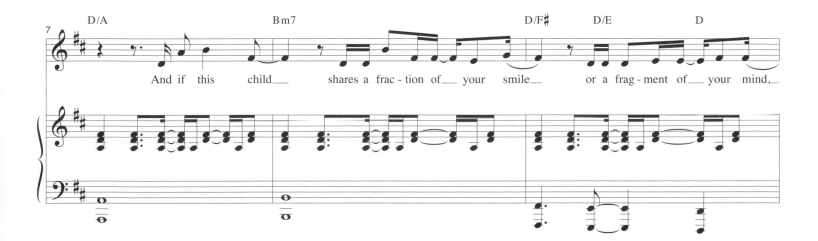

look out, world!__ That would be e-nough. I don't pre-tend__ to know__ the chal-leng-es__ you're fac-

- ing. The worlds you keep__ e-ras - ing and__ cre-at - ing in__ your mind.__ But I'm not a-fraid.__

I know__ who I mar-ried. __ So long as you come home at the end of the day, that would be e-nough.

We don't__ need a leg-a-cy.__ We don't__ need mon-ey.__ If I could grant you peace__ of mind,__

HISTORY HAS ITS EYES ON YOU

Words and Music by LIN-MANUEL MIRANDA
Arranged by Alex Lacamoire and Lin-Manuel Miranda

I was young-er than you are now___ when I was giv-en my first com-mand.

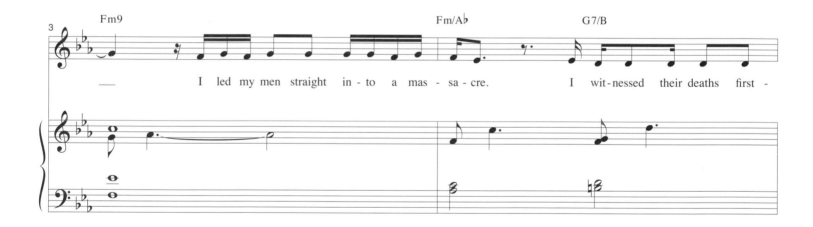

___ I led my men straight in-to a mas-sa-cre. I wit-nessed their deaths first-

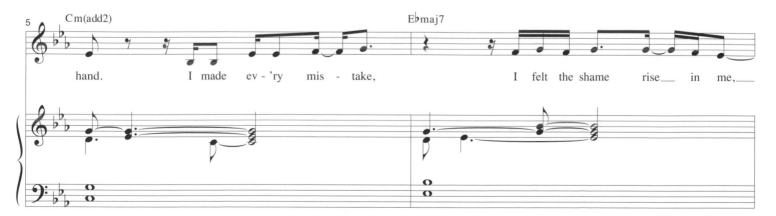

hand. I made ev-'ry mis-take, I felt the shame rise___ in me,

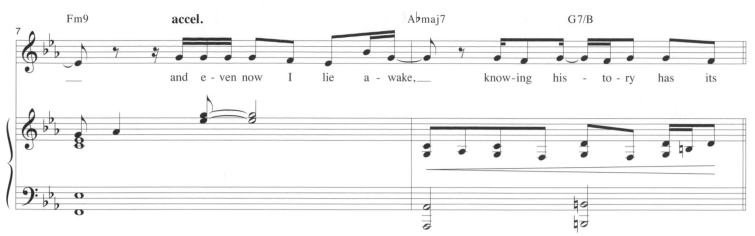

and e-ven now I lie a-wake,___ know-ing his-to-ry has its

A little faster; steady (♩ = 78)

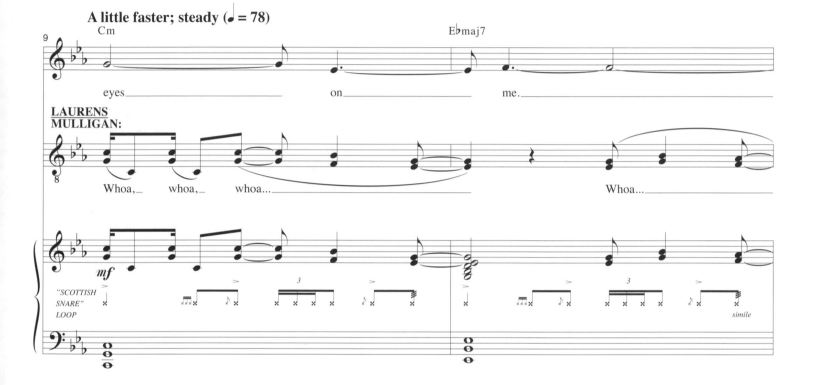

eyes___ on___ me.___

LAURENS
MULLIGAN:

Whoa,___ whoa,___ whoa...___ Whoa...___

"SCOTTISH SNARE" LOOP

simile

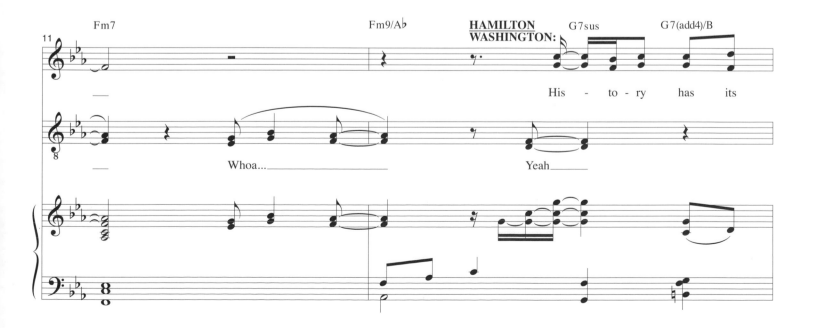

___ His-to-ry has its

Whoa...___ Yeah___

eyes_____ on_____ me._____

COMPANY:
Whoa,___ whoa,___ whoa…_____ Whoa…_____

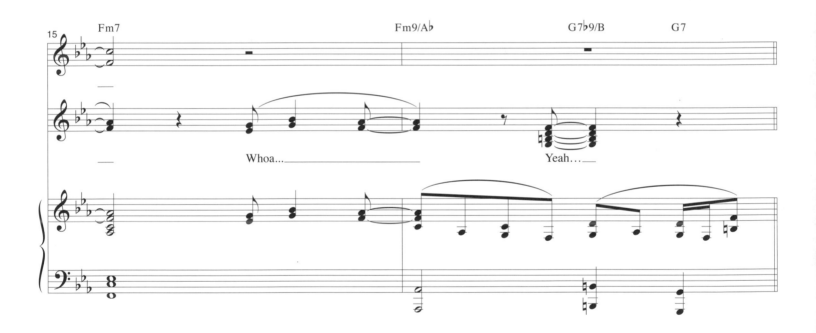

Whoa…_____ Yeah…___

WASHINGTON:
Let me tell you what I wish I'd known___ when I was young and dreamed__ of glo -

- ry: You have no con - trol who lives, who dies, who tells your sto -

WOMEN:
Who lives, who dies, who tells your sto -

MEN:

play if needed

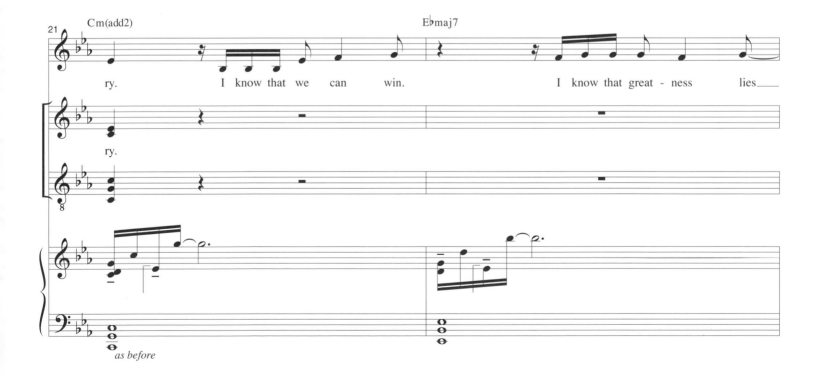

- ry. I know that we can win. I know that great - ness lies___

ry.

ry.

as before

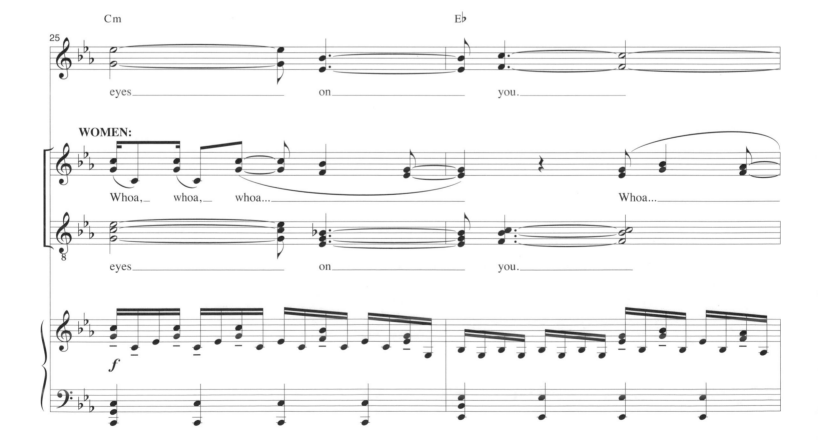

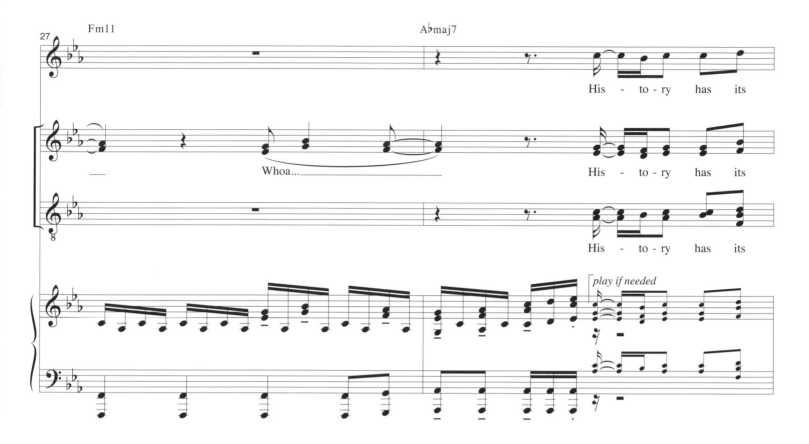

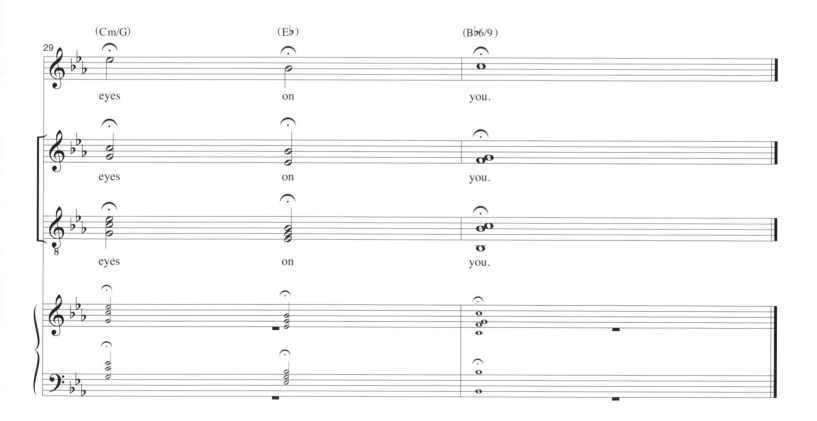

DEAR THEODOSIA

Words and Music by LIN-MANUEL MIRANDA
Arranged by Alex Lacamoire and Lin-Manuel Miranda

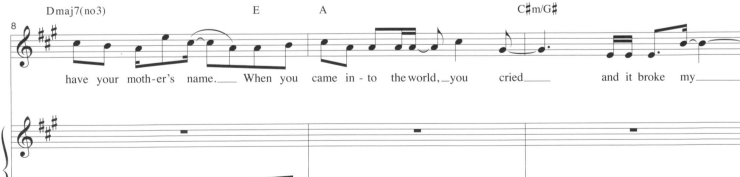

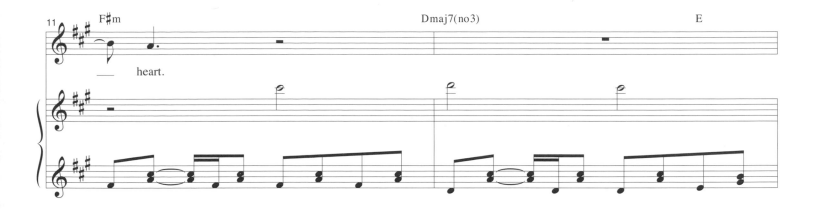

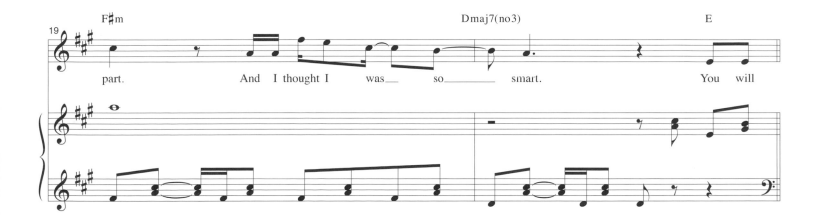

come of age__ with our young na - tion. We'll bleed and fight for you,__ we'll make it

right for you.__ If we lay a strong e - nough__ foun - da - tion we'll pass it

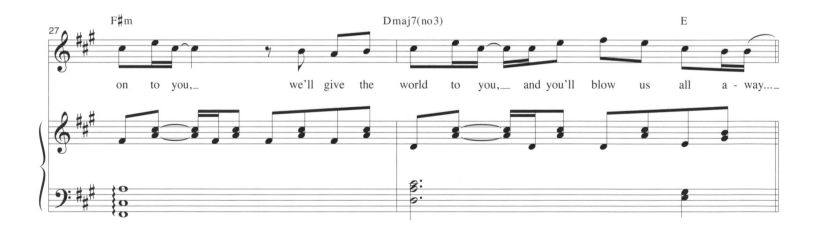

on to you,__ we'll give the world to you,__ and you'll blow us all a - way....

__ some - day, some - day.__

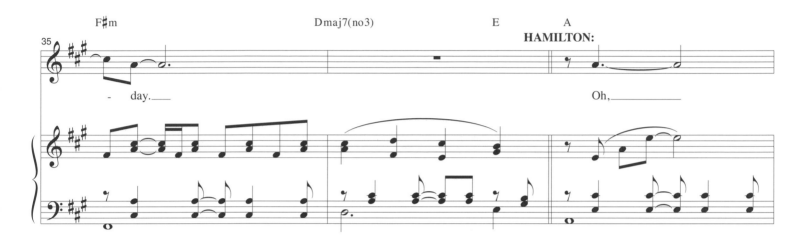

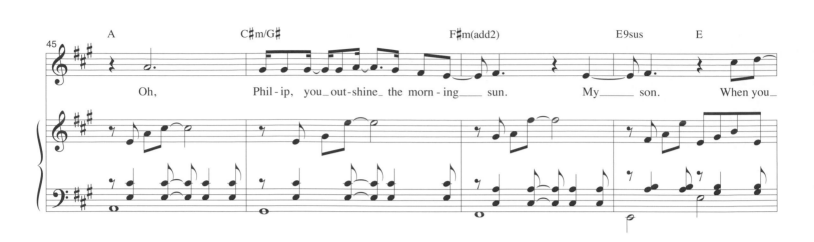

Oh, Phil-ip, you out-shine the morn-ing sun. My son. When you

smile, I fall a-part. And I thought I was so smart.

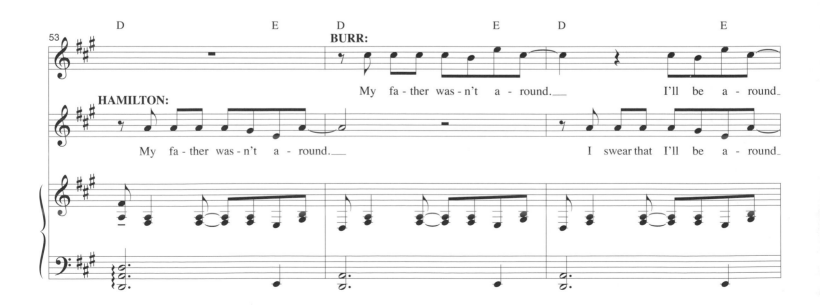

BURR: My fa-ther was-n't a-round. I'll be a-round

HAMILTON: My fa-ther was-n't a-round. I swear that I'll be a-round

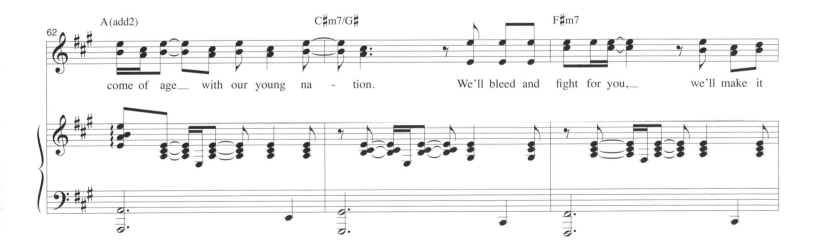

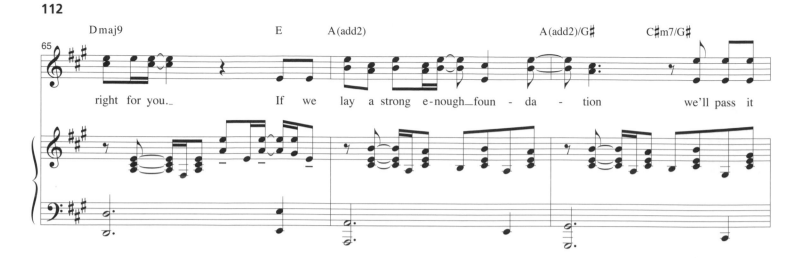

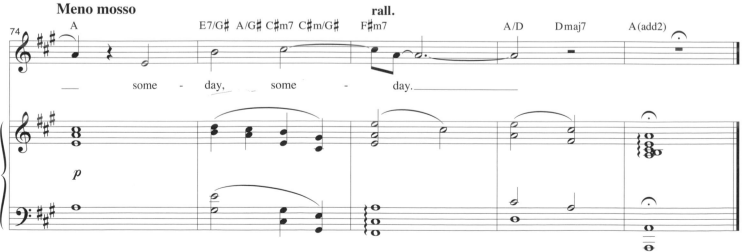

WHAT'D I MISS

Words and Music by LIN-MANUEL MIRANDA
Arranged by Alex Lacamoire and Lin-Manuel Miranda

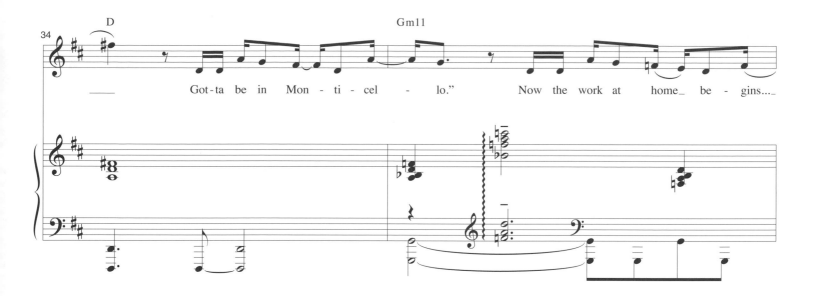

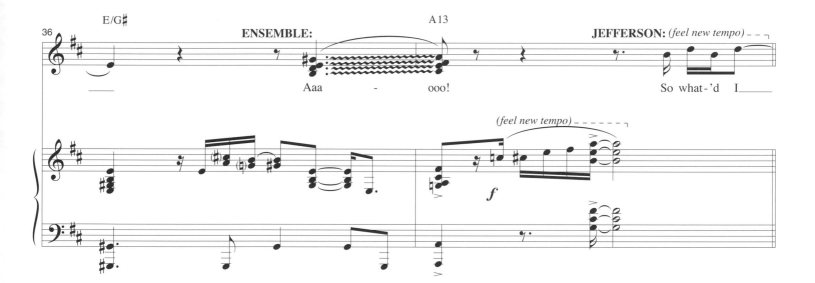

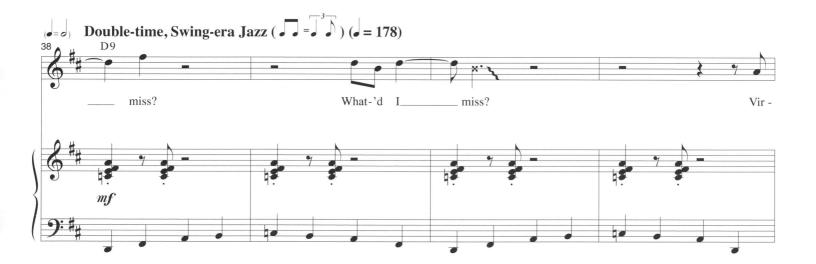

gin-ia, my home sweet home,__ I wan-na give you a kiss.__ I've been in

Par-is meet-ing lots of dif-f'rent la-dies. I guess I ba-sic-'lly missed__ the late eight-ies. I trav-eled the

wide wide__ world__ and came back to this...__

ENSEMBLE: Aa -

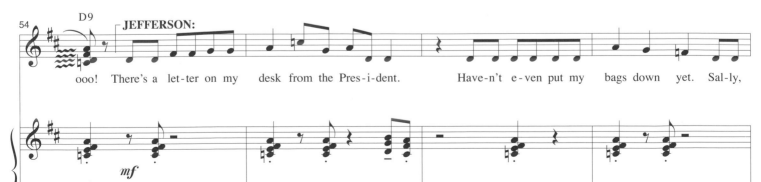

ooo! There's a let-ter on my desk from the Pres-i-dent. Have-n't e-ven put my bags down yet. Sal-ly,

JEFFERSON:

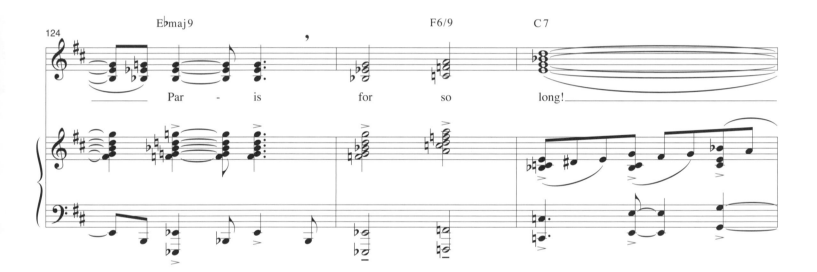

THE ROOM WHERE IT HAPPENS

Words and Music by LIN-MANUEL MIRANDA
Arranged by Alex Lacamoire and Lin-Manuel Miranda

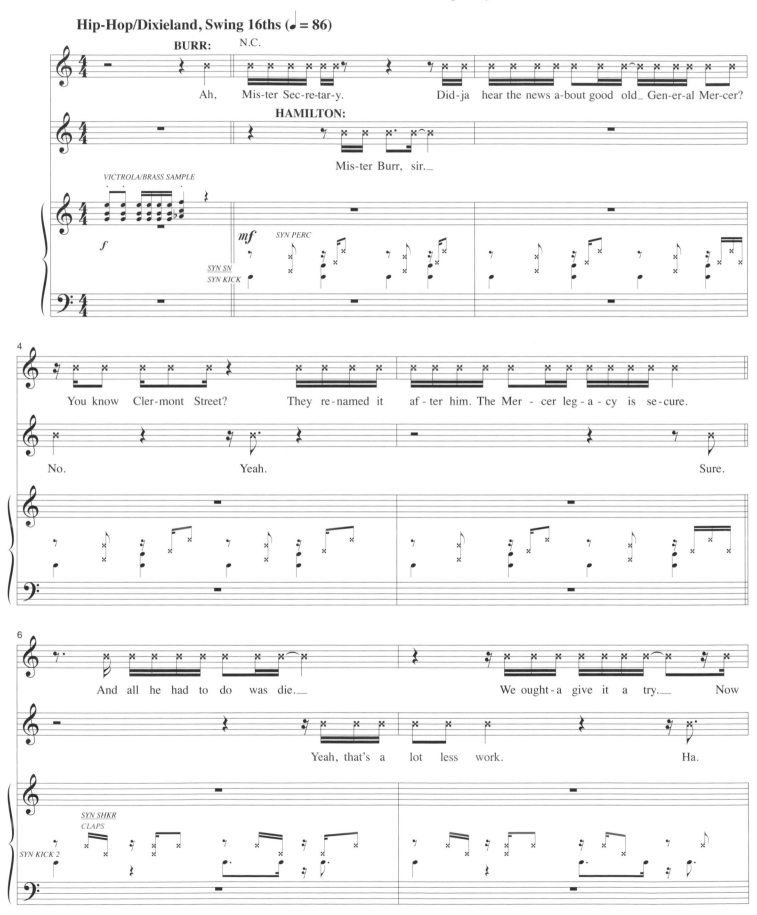

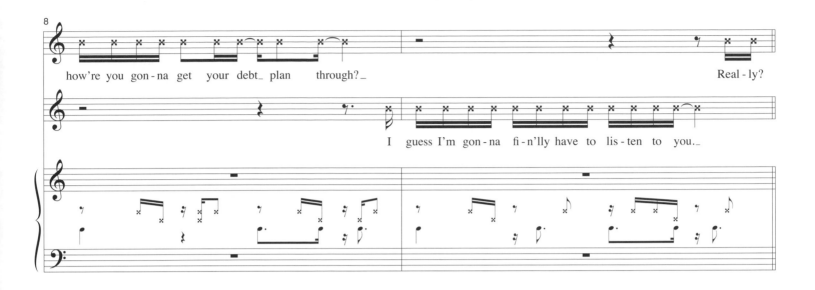

how're you gon-na get your debt plan through? Real-ly?

I guess I'm gon-na fi-n'lly have to lis-ten to you.

Am(add2)   Am(add2)/F   Cmaj7(no3)/E♭   Cmaj7(no3)/D   Cmaj7(no3)/G

Ha.

Talk   less.   Smile_____ more.

hold R.H. notes into each other

mf

SYN PERC

SYN SN
SYN KICK

simile

Am(add2)   Am(add2)/F   Cmaj7(no3)/E♭   Cmaj7(no3)/D   Cmaj7(no3)/G

Do what-ev-er it takes_ to get___ my plan_____ on the Con - gress___ floor.

Now, Mad - i - son and Jef - fer - son are mer - ci - less.

Well, hate the sin, love the sin - ner.

MADISON: Ham - il - ton!

BURR: But—

I'm sor - ry, Burr, I've got - ta go.

De - ci - sions are hap - pen - ing o - ver din - ner.

BURR: Two Vir - gin - ians and an im - mi - grant walk in - to a room. Di - a - met - ri - c'lly op - posed, foes.

ENSEMBLE: Di - a - met - ri - c'lly op - posed, foes.

drums/perc continue as before

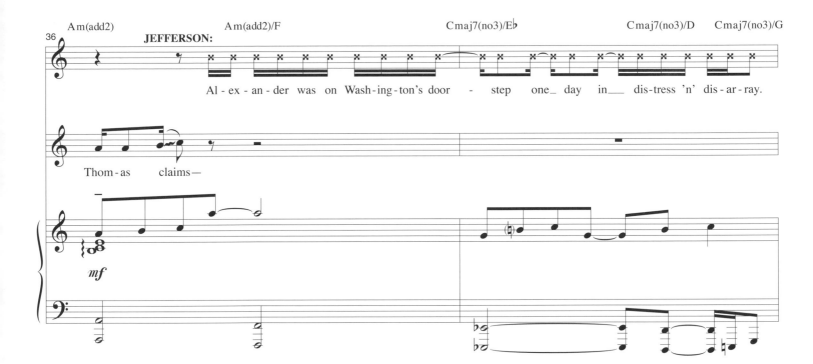

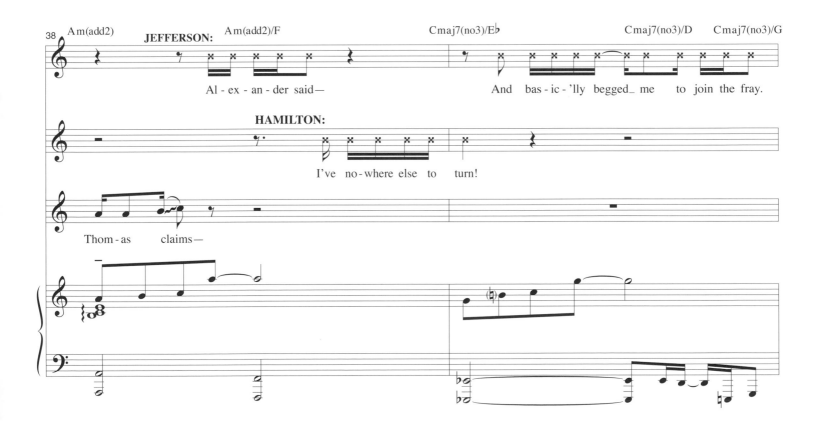

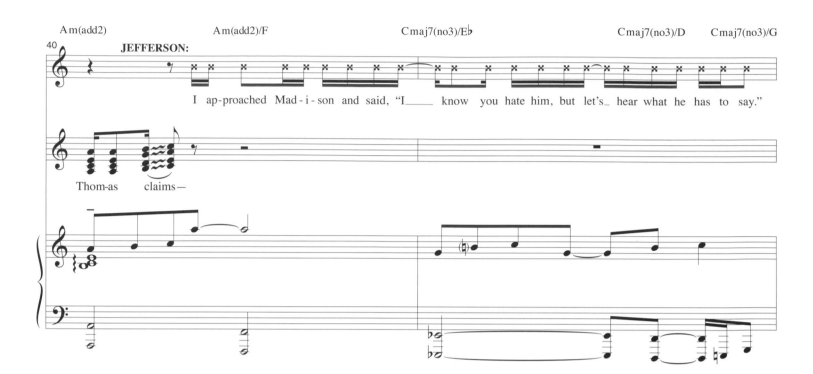

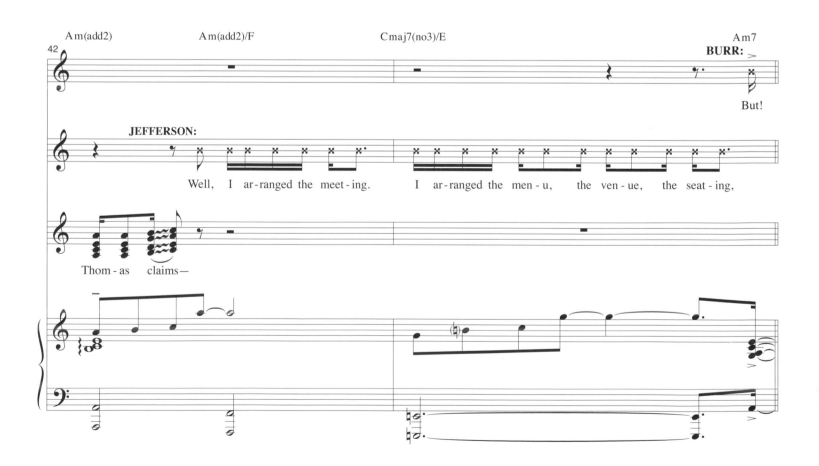

Jef - fer - son ap-proach-es with a din-ner and in - vite, and Mad-i-son re-sponds with Vir-gin-i-an in - sight:

MADISON:
May-be we can solve one prob-lem with an-oth-er and win a vic-to-ry for the South-ern-ers, in oth-er words—

JEFFERSON:
Oh -

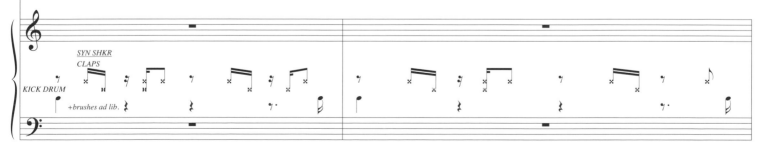

A *quid pro quo.* Would - n't you like to work a lit - tle clos - er to home?_

ho! I sup - pose._ Ac - tual -

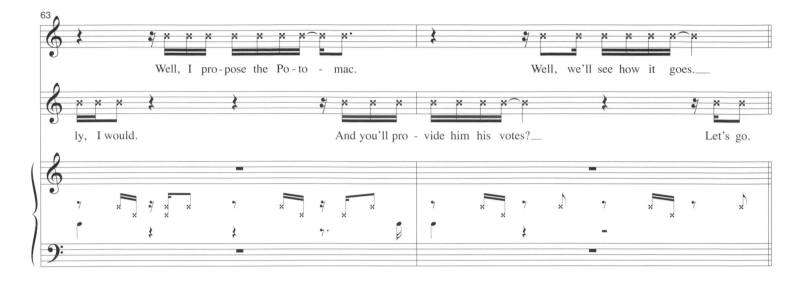

63

Well, I pro-pose the Po-to - mac.

Well, we'll see how it goes.___

ly, I would.

And you'll pro - vide him his votes?___

Let's go.

65 **BURR:**

F9   D9   Bdim7   E7♭9 Am/E

Noooo...

The room where it hap-pened. The room where it hap-pened.

ENS:

—one else was in the room where it hap-pened. The room where it hap-pened. The room where it hap-pened.

(mute)   *f*

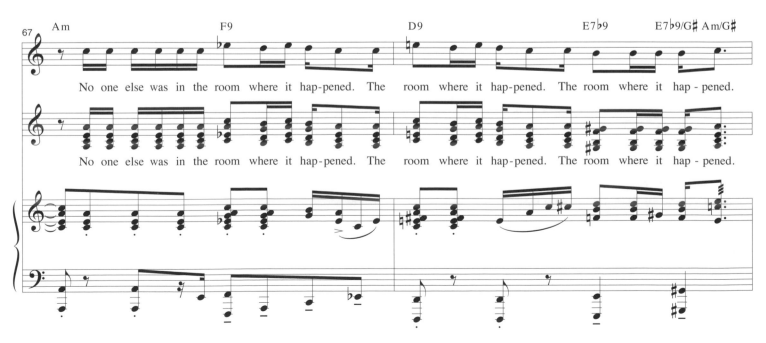

67 Am   F9   D9   E7♭9   E7♭9/G♯ Am/G♯

No one else was in the room where it hap-pened. The room where it hap-pened. The room where it hap-pened.

No one else was in the room where it hap-pened. The room where it hap-pened. The room where it hap-pened.

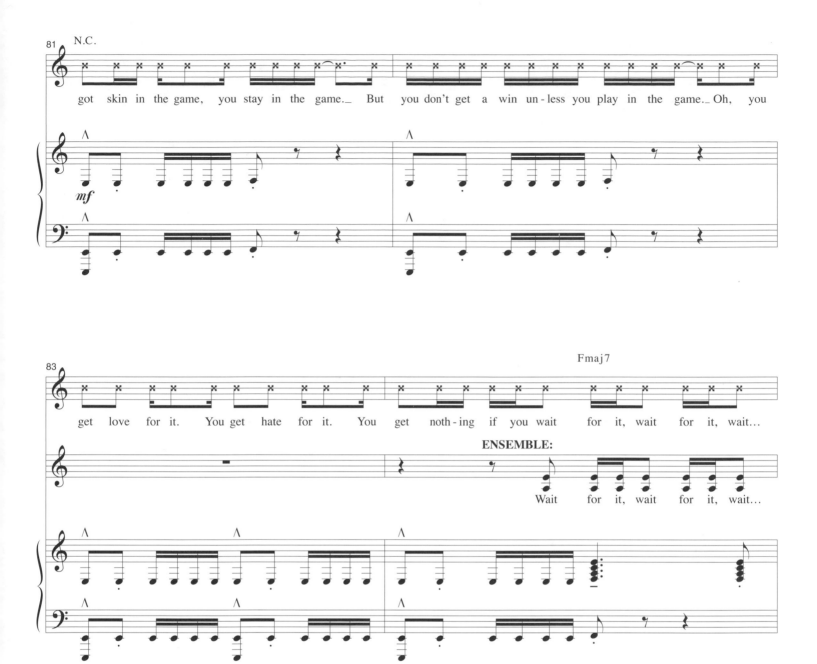

got skin in the game, you stay in the game.__ But you don't get a win un-less you play in the game.__ Oh, you

get love for it. You get hate for it. You get noth-ing if you wait for it, wait for it, wait...

ENSEMBLE:

Wait for it, wait for it, wait...

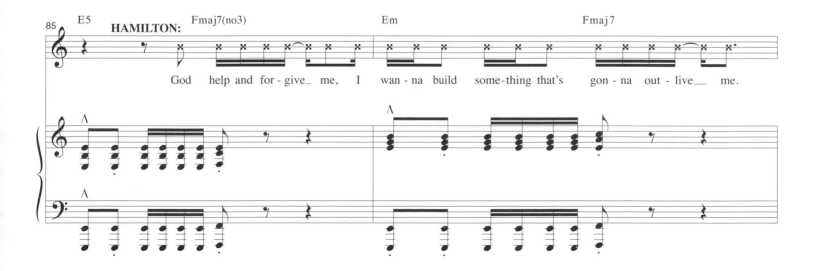

HAMILTON:

God help and for-give__ me, I wan-na build some-thing that's gon-na out-live__ me.

accel. poco a poco

Tempo I

hard accents on 2&4 (a strong backbeat)

oh,_____ oh!_____ I wan-na be, I wan-na be in... I've got_

I wan-na be in the room where it hap-pens. The room where it hap-pens. The room where it hap-pens.

___ to be, I've got__ to be_____ in__ the room, in that big ol'__ room!_____

I wan-na be in the room where it hap-pens. The room where it hap-pens. The room where it hap-pens.

_____ Hold your nose and close your eyes.___

ENSEMBLE:

The art of the com - pro - mise—___

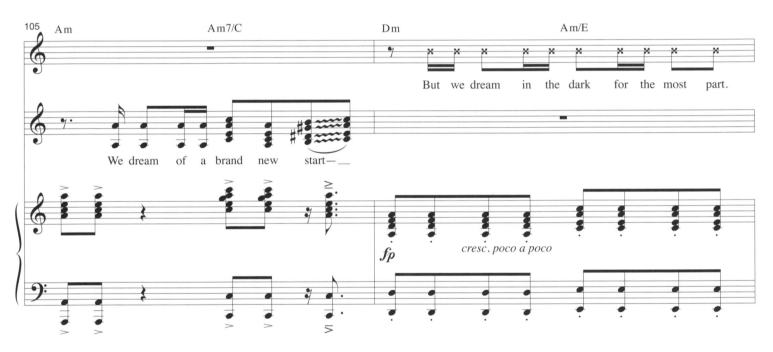

WASHINGTON ON YOUR SIDE

Words and Music by LIN-MANUEL MIRANDA
Arranged by Alex Lacamoire and Lin-Manuel Miranda

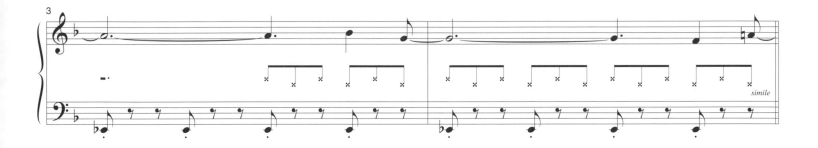

Try not to crack un - der the stress, we're break - ing down like frac - tions.

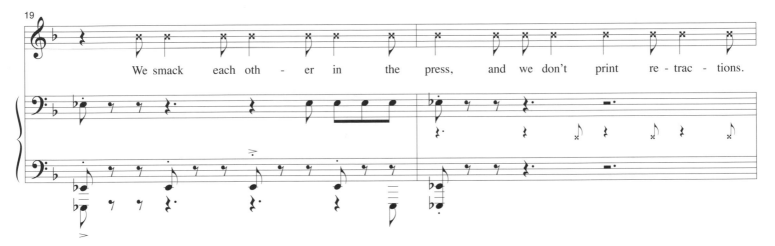

We smack each oth - er in the press, and we don't print re - trac - tions.

I get no sat - is - fac - tion wit - ness - ing his fits of pas - sion.

simile

The way he primps and preens and dress - es like the pits of fash - ion.

Our poor - est cit - i - zens,__ our farm - ers, live ra - tion to ra - tion

as Wall Street robs 'em blind in search of chips to cash in.

CLAPS

This prick is ask - in' for some-one to bring him to task.

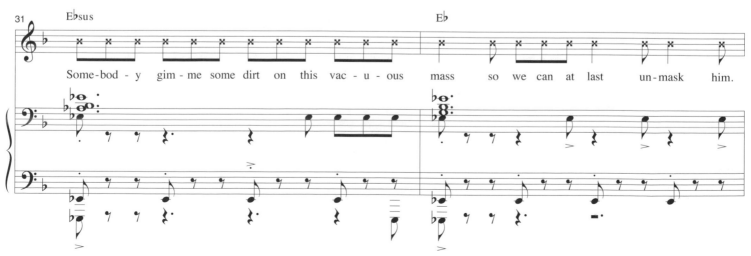

Some-bod - y gim-me some dirt on this vac-u-ous mass so we can at last un-mask him.

I'll pull the trig-ger on him, some-one load the gun and cock it.

While we were all watch-ing, he got Wash-ing-ton in his pock-et.

BURR
JEFFERSON:

It must___ be nice, it must___ be nice___

___ to have Wash-ing-ton on___ your___ side._

It must___ be nice, it must___ be nice___

to have Wash - ing - ton on___ your___ side.

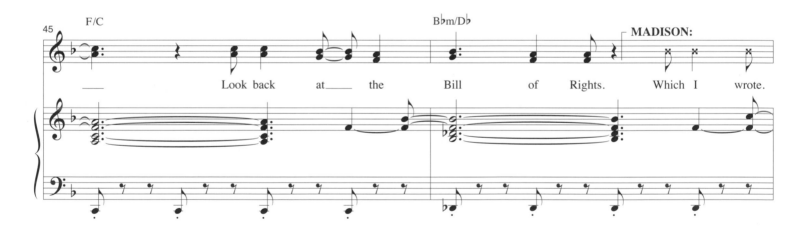

F/C

B♭m/D♭

MADISON:

Look back at___ the Bill of Rights. Which I wrote.

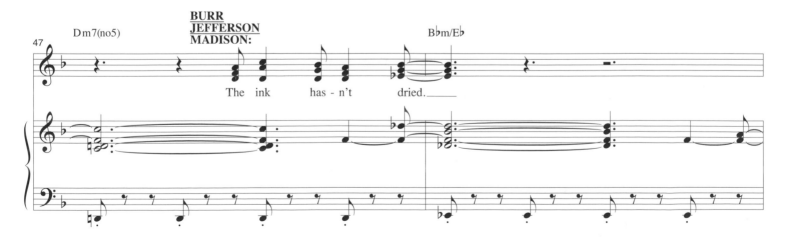

Dm7(no5)

BURR
JEFFERSON
MADISON:

B♭m/E♭

The ink has - n't dried.___

It must_ be nice, it must_ be nice_

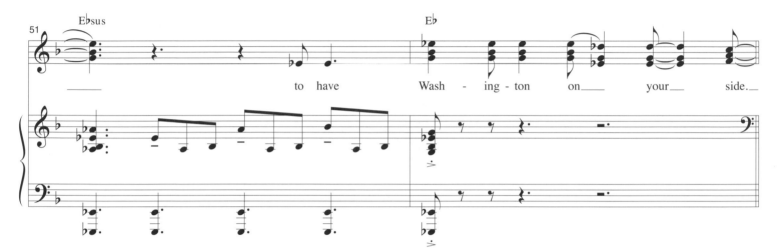

_____ to have Wash - ing - ton on_ your_ side._

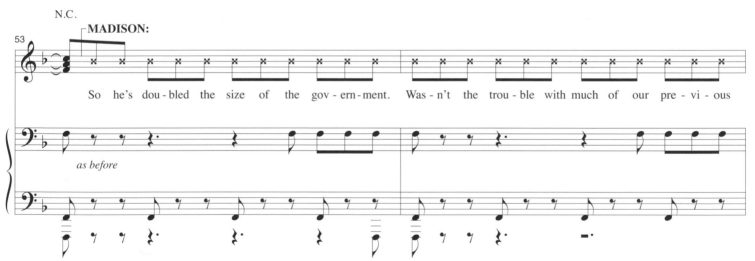

MADISON: So he's dou-bled the size of the gov-ern-ment. Was-n't the trou-ble with much of our pre-vi-ous

as before

gov - ern - ment size? **BURR:** Look in his eyes! **JEFFERSON:** See how he lies. **MADISON:** Fol - low the scent of his

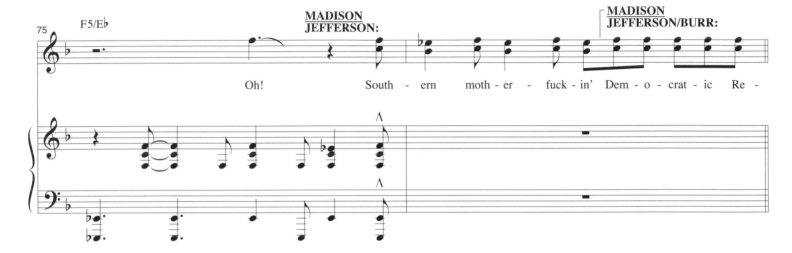

ENSEMBLE: Oh!

MADISON JEFFERSON/BURR: If we fol-low the mon-ey and see where it leads____

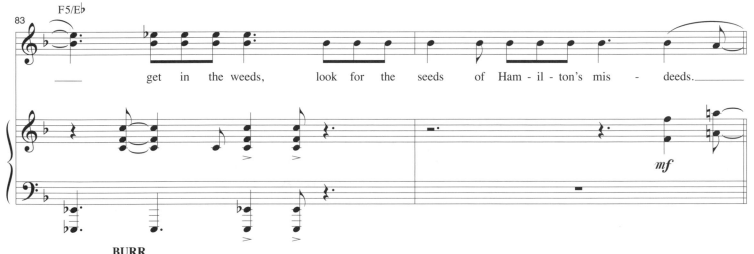

____ get in the weeds, look for the seeds of Ham-il-ton's mis - deeds.____

BURR JEFFERSON MADISON: It must____ be nice, it must____ be nice.____

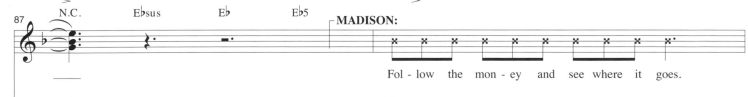

MADISON: Fol-low the mon-ey and see where it goes.

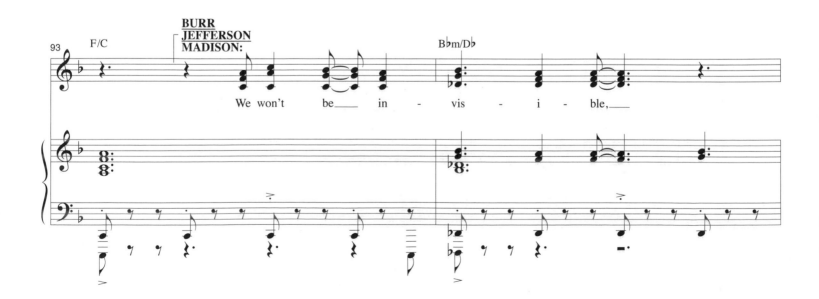

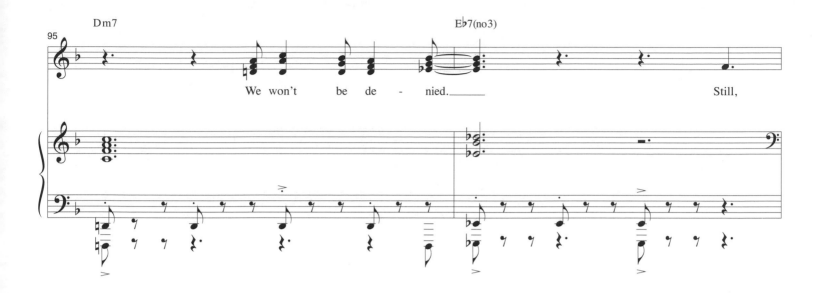

We won't be de - nied._____ Still,

it must__ be nice, it must__ be nice_____

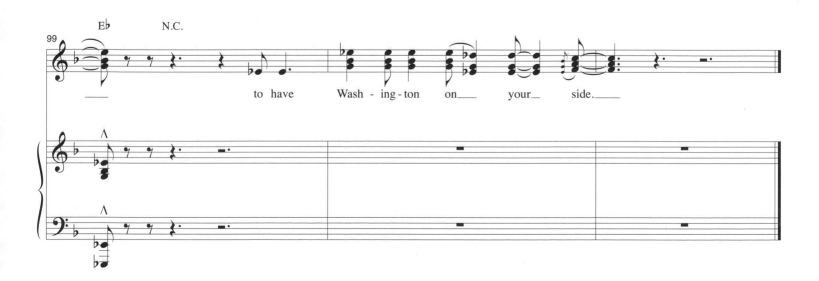

____ to have Wash - ing - ton on__ your__ side._____

ONE LAST TIME

Words and Music by LIN-MANUEL MIRANDA
Arranged by Alex Lacamoire and Lin-Manuel Miranda

I need you to draft an ad-dress.

No,

Yes! He re-signed. You can fin-'lly speak your mind—

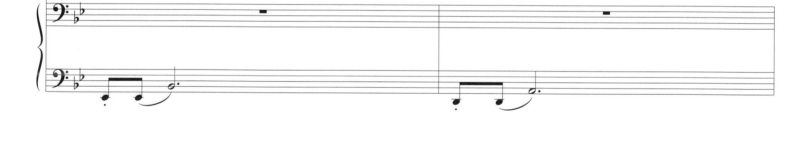

he's step-ping down so he can run for pres-i-dent.

Ha! Good luck de-feat-ing you, sir.

I'm step-ping down. I'm not running for pres-i-dent.

I'm sor-ry, what?

talk a-bout what I have learned.___ The hard - won wis - dom I have earned.___

HAMILTON:
As far as the peo -

- ple are___ con - cerned,___ you have___ to serve, you could___ con - tin - ue to serve___

No!

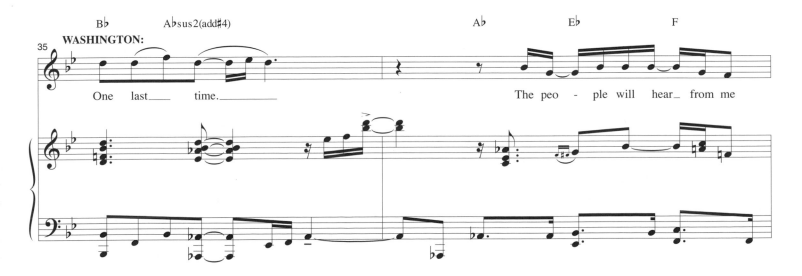

WASHINGTON:
One last___ time.___

The peo - ple will hear___ from me

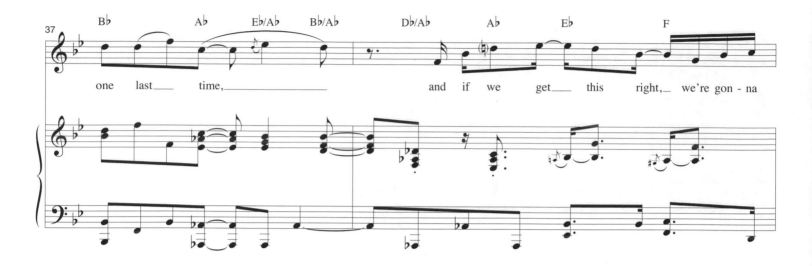

one last____ time,_____ and if we get____ this right,__ we're gon - na

teach 'em how to say____ good - bye,_____ you____ and I.____

HAMILTON:

Mis - ter

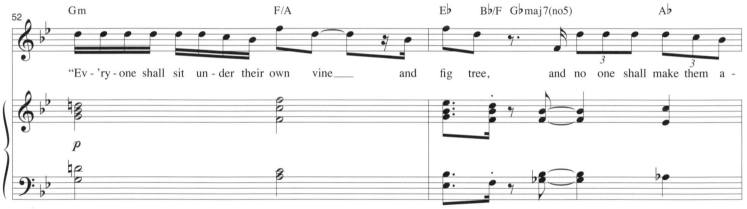

A little slower, steady, straight 16ths

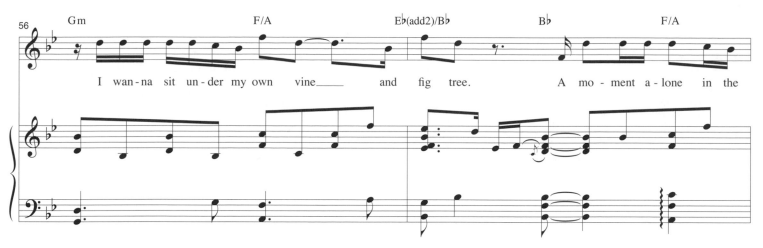

I wan-na sit un-der my own vine____ and fig tree. A mo-ment a-lone in the

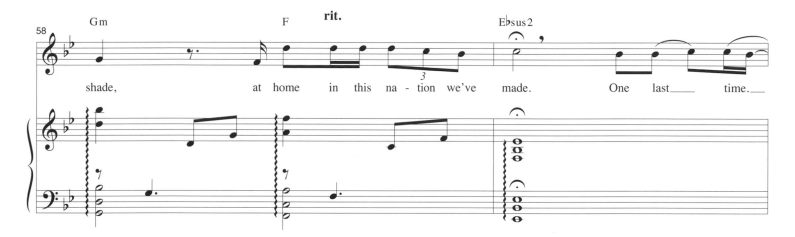

shade, at home in this na-tion we've made. One last____ time.____

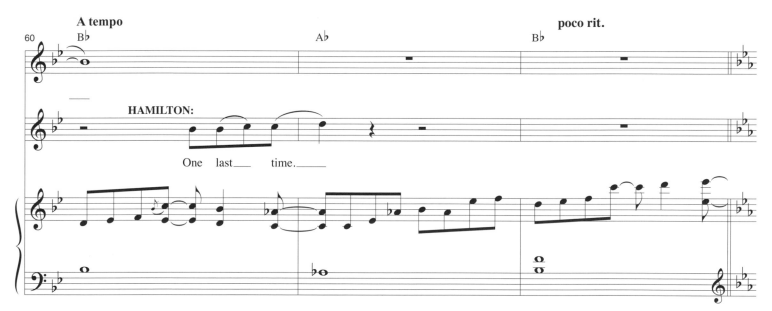

HAMILTON:

One last____ time.____

HAMILTON: "Though, in reviewing the incidents of my administration, I am unconscious of intentional error, I am nevertheless too sensible of my defects not to think it probable that I may have committed many errors."

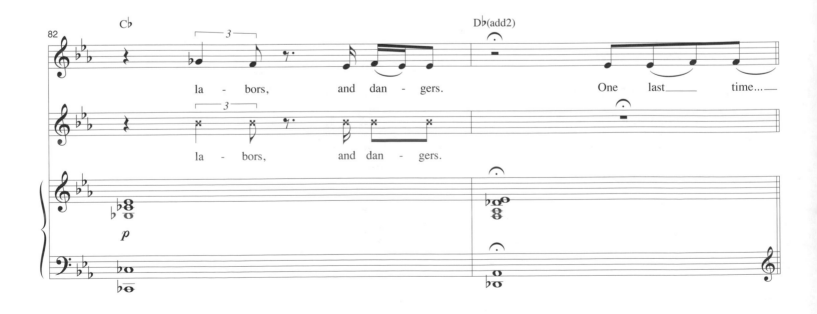

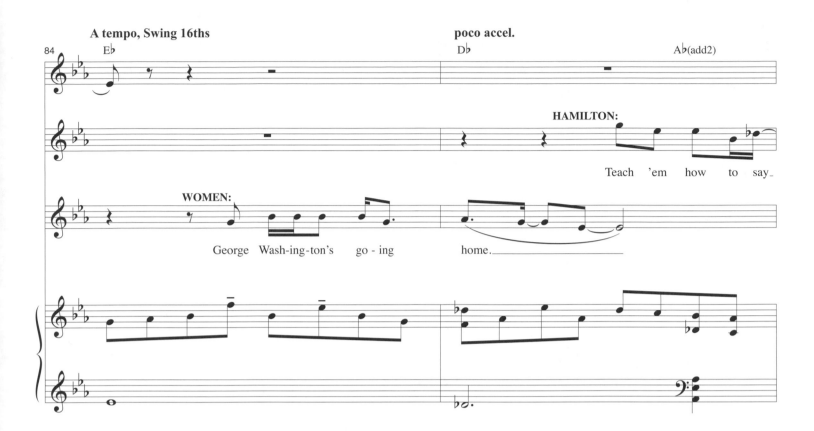

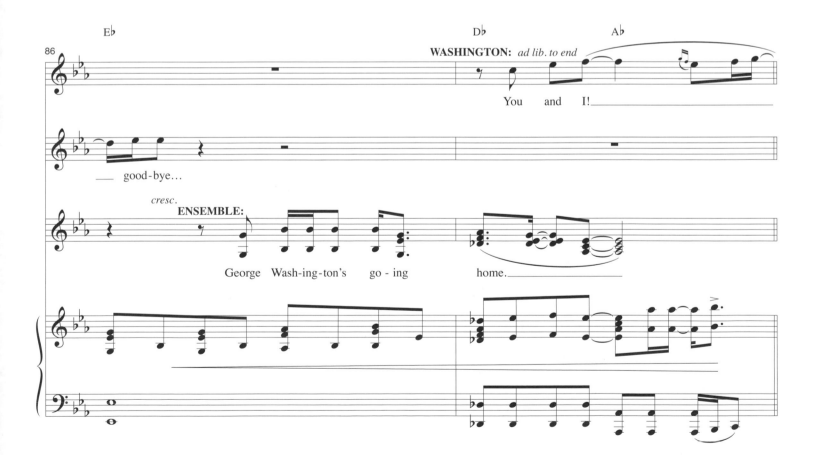

HURRICANE

Words and Music by LIN-MANUEL MIRANDA
Arranged by Alex Lacamoire and Lin-Manuel Miranda

HAMILTON: In the eye of a hur-ri-cane there is qui - et for just a mo - ment, a yel-low sky._ When I was sev-en-teen a hur-ri-cane_ des-troyed my_ town._ I did-n't drown._ I could-n't seem____ to die. I wrote_ my way

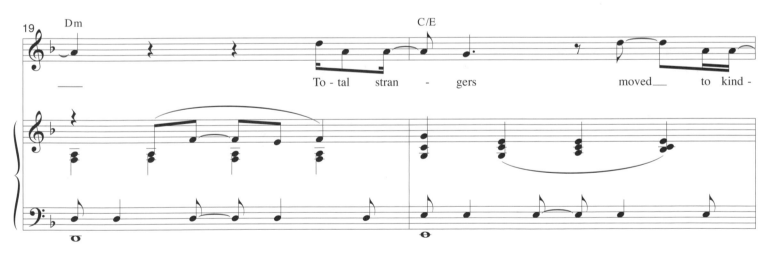

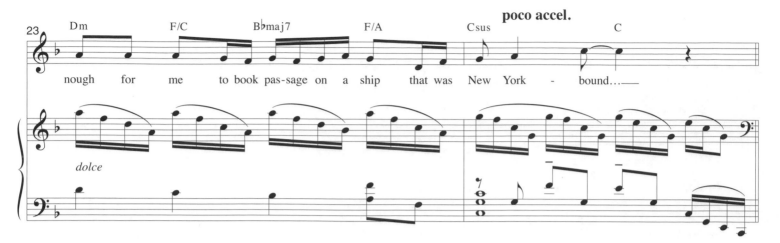

poco accel.

Dm   F/C   B♭maj7   F/A   Csus   C

nough for me to book pas-sage on a ship that was New York - bound...

dolce

Più mosso (♩=87)

D5   F5   G5   A5   C5   D5

I wrote my way out of hell._ I wrote my way to rev-o - lu-tion. I was loud-er than the crack in the bell._ I wrote E-

dry

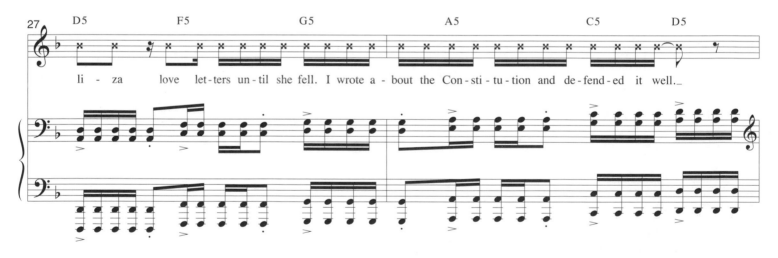

D5   F5   G5   A5   C5   D5

li - za love let-ters un-til she fell. I wrote a - bout the Con-sti - tu - tion and de-fend-ed it well._

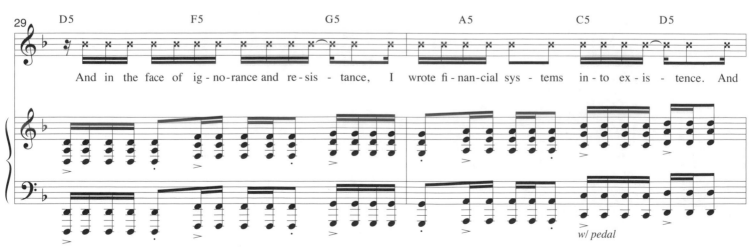

D5   F5   G5   A5   C5   D5

And in the face of ig-no-rance and re-sis - tance, I wrote fi-nan-cial sys - tems in-to ex - is - tence. And

w/ pedal

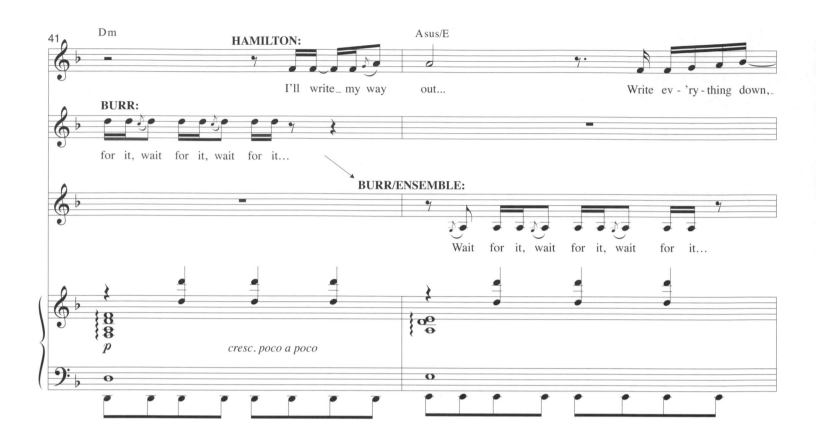

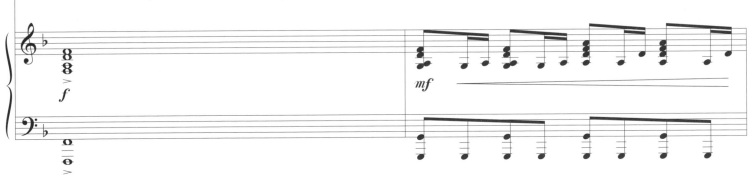

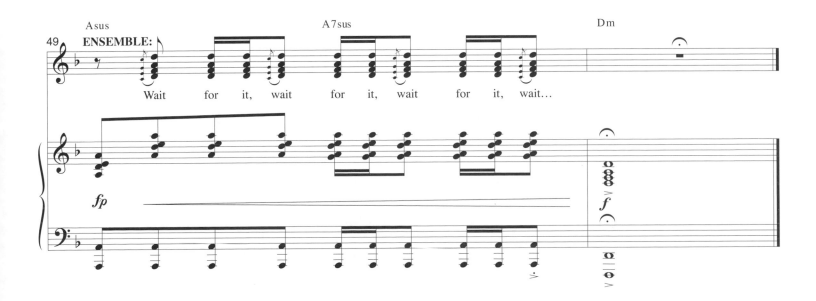

BURN

Words and Music by LIN-MANUEL MIRANDA
Arranged by Alex Lacamoire and Lin-Manuel Miranda

saved ev-'ry let-ter you wrote me.___ From the mo-ment I read them I knew you were

mine. You said you were mine. I thought you were___ mine.___

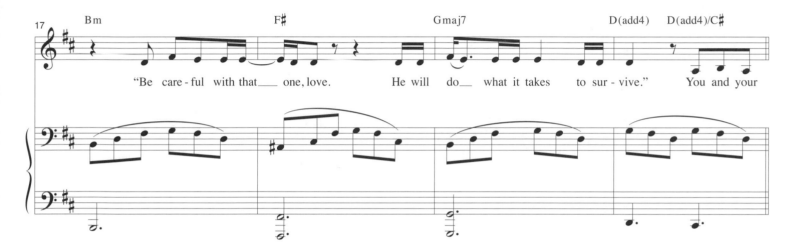

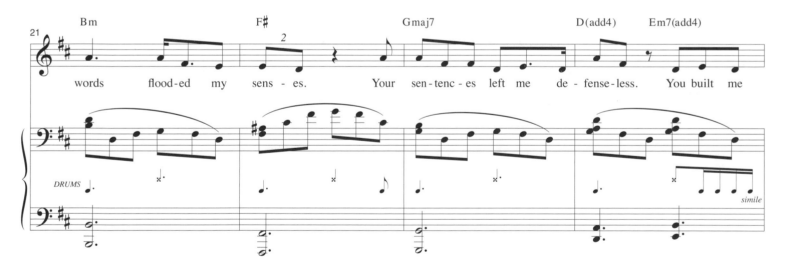

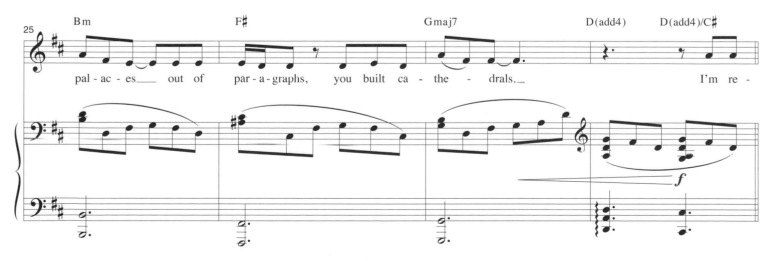

pub-lished the let-ters she wrote you.__ You told the whole world how you brought this girl in-to our

bed. In clear-ing your name, you have ru-ined our_____ lives._____

Do you know what An - gel-i-ca said when she read what you'd done? She said,

"You have mar-ried an Ic - a-rus. He has flown__ too close to the sun." You and your

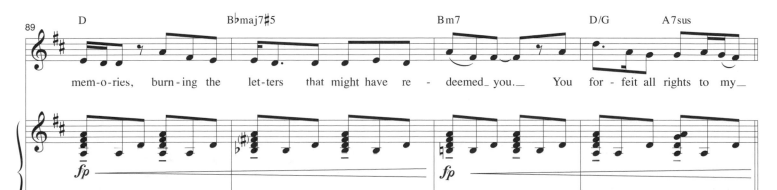

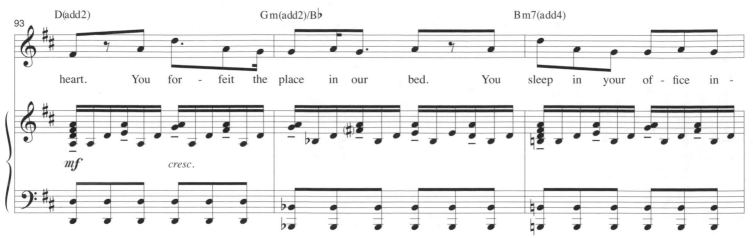

heart. You for - feit the place in our bed. You sleep in your of - fice in -

stead, with on - ly___ the mem-o-ries of when you were___ mine.___

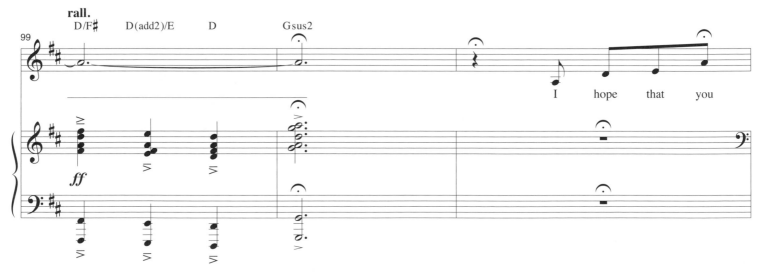

I hope that you

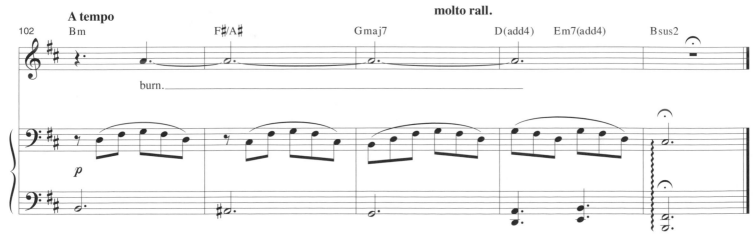

burn.

IT'S QUIET UPTOWN

Words and Music by LIN-MANUEL MIRANDA
Arranged by Alex Lacamoire and Lin-Manuel Miranda

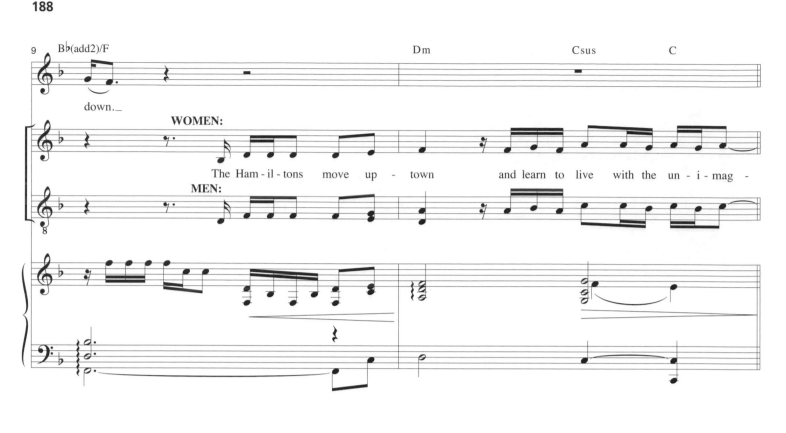

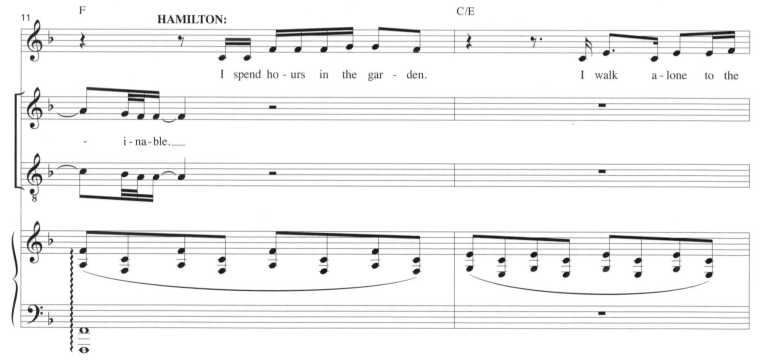

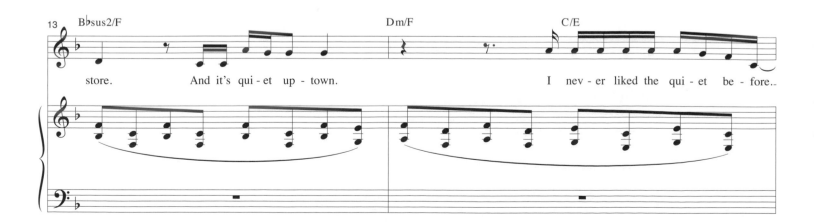

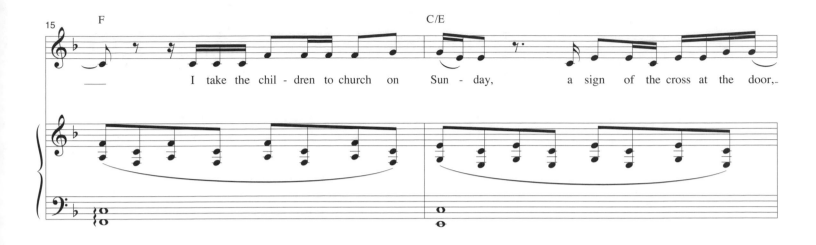

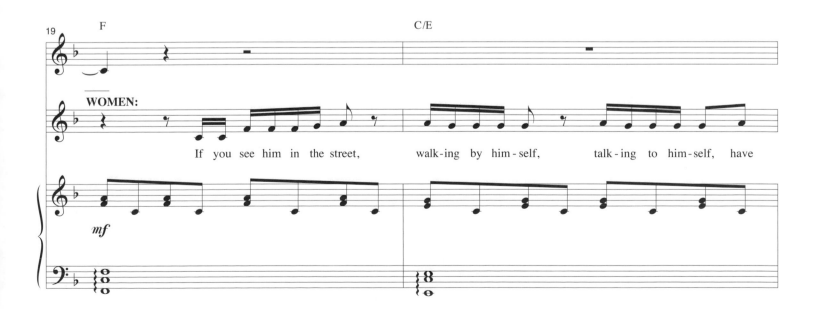

MEN sound one octave lower.

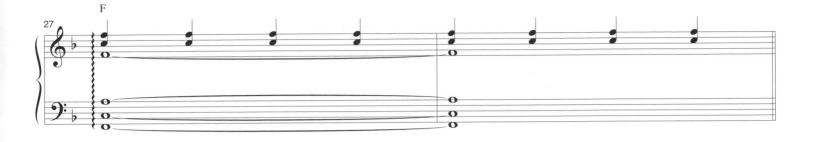

HAMILTON:
Look at where we are.___ Look at where we start - ed.___

I know I don't de-serve you, E - li - za. But hear me out. That would be e - nough.

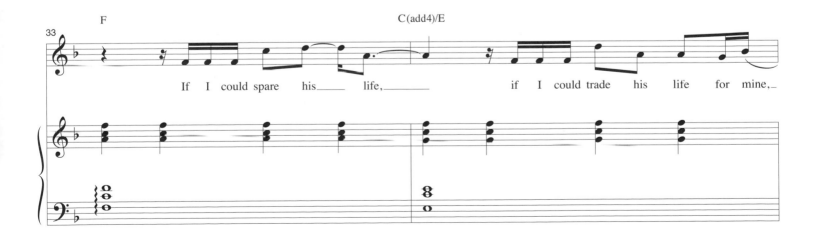

If I could spare his___ life,___ if I could trade his life for mine,___

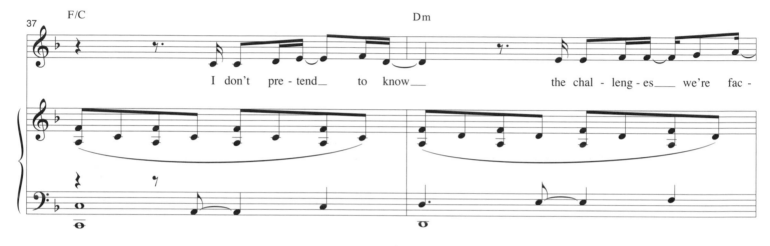

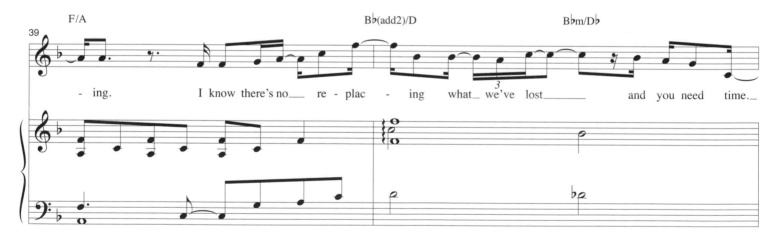

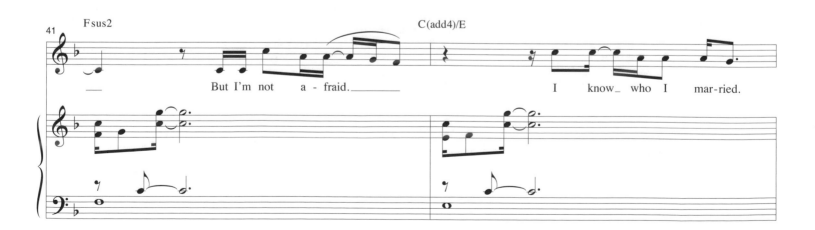

Just let me stay here by___ your side._____ That would be e - nough.

WOMEN:
If you see him in the street, walk-ing by her side, talk-ing by her side, have

MEN:

HAMILTON:
E - li - za, do you like it up - town? It's qui - et up - town.

pit - y. He is try'ng to do the un - i - mag -

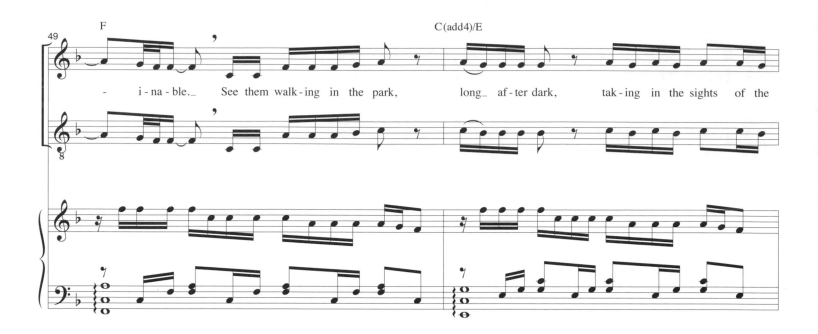

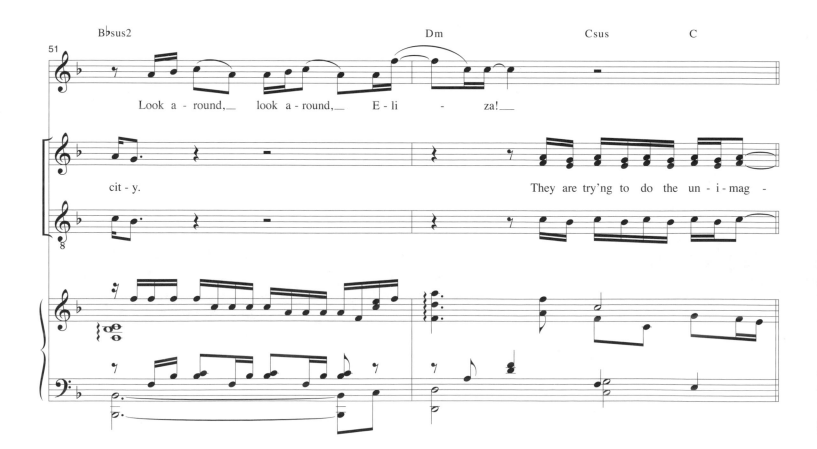

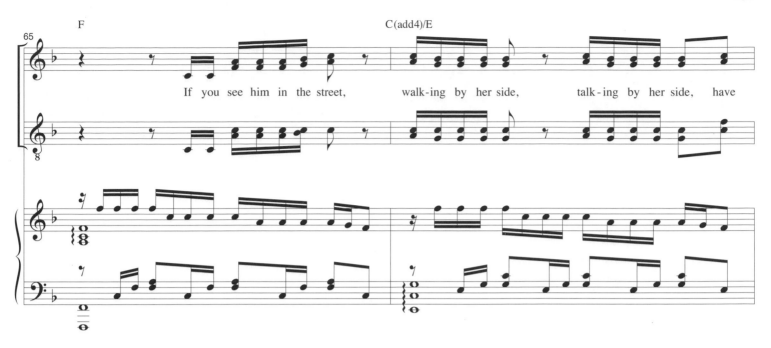

If you see him in the street, walk-ing by her side, talk-ing by her side, have

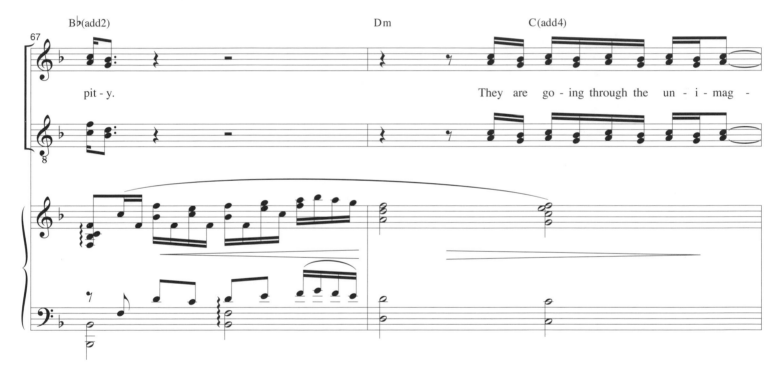

pit - y. They are go - ing through the un - i - mag -

molto rall.

- i - na - ble.